MW01687344

COOKING WITH YOGURT

by Carol LeHeup

ACKNOWLEDGEMENTS

Thanks particularly to the Ormiston Family (owners of Olympic Dairy Products Ltd.) for participating in taste tests, always being positive, helpful and encouraging and for supplying all the yogurt.

Flowers

The arrangement featured on Page 161, with Hungarian Goulash Soup, was donated by Flowers & Co., White Rock, B.C.

Photography

The photographers for the six colored pictures were Diane Morrison and Stephen Lowe.

Publishing

Carol LeHeup with computer assistance from my brother, Bruce Helmer.

Printer

Peace Arch Printing, White Rock, B.C.

Props for Pictures

Thanks to my mother, Emelie Helmer; my sister, Ellen deBruyn; and friends Carol Jensen, Vivian Swaré, Ellen Tozer, Lorna Harvey and the Ormistons.

Recipes

Thanks to my friends, family and co-workers who shared their favorite yogurt recipes. A special thanks to Penny Arden of Victoria, B.C. who tested a number of recipes.

Tasters

Thanks to my family, friends, neighbors and co-workers for their constructive criticism at dinner parties, coffee breaks and taste tests so this book could become a reality.

Thanks to my preschooler "buddies" in the neighborhood for testing the yogurt popsicles and muffins. They gave them the "seal of approval" and want me to do another book so they can help again.

TABLE OF CONTENTS

INTRODUCTION

It has been alot of fun "Cooking with Yogurt"!

There have been fun dinner parties, taste tests and samplings. Whenever I had to bring a dish to a potluck or dinner party, everyone knew there would be a new yogurt dish to try. Friends liked being involved and giving their opinion as to whether or not it should be included in "The Book"! There were very few recipes that were totally rejected. If I thought a recipe still had potential, it was back to the kitchen to experiment some more.

I have tried to keep the recipes uncomplicated and straight forward so you will enjoy "Cooking with Yogurt", too, particularly the "eating" part. As well as most of the recipes being quick and easy to prepare on a daily basis, they will also be welcome additions at your 'special' dinners.

Creating this book was interesting because previously I was not a yogurt "fan" and I had never used yogurt in cooking. But because I am always interested in trying new recipes, I thought it would be a fun learning experience... and it was! Besides, yogurt is good for you and has less calories then sour cream and mayonnaise and more food value than milk!

There were many other gratifying discoveries as well. The meatloaf is very moist with the addition of yogurt as are the muffins and bread. Sauces have an extra special taste with the added tang of yogurt. Try the recipes. You will be pleasantly surprised!

I found the unflavored Olympic Natural Yogurt, 2% Yogurt and Skim Milk Yogurt to be completely interchangeable in recipes so if you are counting calories and watching the fat content, you may want to use skim milk yogurt or 2%.

Welcome to the wonderful world of "Cooking with Yogurt"! I hope you will enjoy it!

Carol LeHeup

The History of Yogurt

No one knows exactly how or when yogurt was discovered. There are references in the Bible to it being used by Abraham and Moses. Homer sang its praises in the "Iliad". Desert nomads packed their yogurt cultures along with their camels, wives and tents when they changed oases. The fact is that yogurt is over 4,000 years old. While we, in North America, have just started to savor its tart taste and virtues, the people of Eastern Europe have been doing so for thousands of years.

The man most responsible for taking yogurt from the nomadic goatskin bag and putting it onto the 20th Century table was a Russian scientist, Dr. Ilya Metchnikoff. A Nobel prize winner and member of the Pasteur Institute of Paris, he is also author of "The Prolongation of Life", "Old Age", and "The Nature of Man". His research into the longevity of Bulgarians who consumed large quantities of yogurt led him to believe the two were related.

It has only been in the last couple of decades that North Americans have discovered what the rest of the world has known for 4,000 years...that yogurt tastes as good as it is for you.

It was to satisfy the tastes of North Americans, weaned on sweets, that fruit was added to yogurt. Preserves were put on the bottom of the container and then filled with yogurt which became known as sundae-style yogurt. A later development was swiss-style yogurt where the yogurt and preserves were already blended.

With a renewed health conscientiousness, North Americans are turning to foods that are delicious and nutritious. Yogurt is good for you. This milk culture with its tart, tangy taste has many healthful benefits that have been proven by medical research.

Yogurt and Nutrition

Milk is said to be the closest thing there is to a perfect food. Yogurt, made from milk, has slightly more food value. In the fermentation process, milk sugar (lactose) turns into lactic acid and therefore there is less sugar in yogurt. It is slightly higher in riboflavin and niacin. The bacteria in yogurt more easily synthesize the vitamins in milk, particularly the B complex which is especially important in preventing anemia and nutritional deficiency, making them more readily available to our system. The same is true for the minerals calcium and phosphorus. Yogurt is 'predigested' by its bacteria, therefore it takes only one hour for 90% of the yogurt to be assimilated into the body.

Yogurt can hinder growth of some pathogenic organisms. For example, dysentery bacteria cannot live and develop in an acid medium, neither can Salmonella typhi, the bacteria that cause Samonella.

Food for Medicine

If you integrate yogurt into your diet, supplemented by other healthful and nutritious foods, you'll be further along the way to maintaining good health.

What do medical researchers and doctors say about yogurt and health?

Yogurt and Cholesterol

Dr. George V. Mann: "The Best Medicine for high cholesterol and heart disease comes in a carton, is inexpensive and doesn't have to be prescribed by a Doctor." Yogurt, according to Professor Mann, University of Tennessee, is low in fat and calories and high in calcium and acids which stop the production of cholesterol in the liver.

For people suffering from colitis, yogurt acts as a diuretic and fights fermentation.

As yogurt has a high calcium content, which helps sooth nerves and tense muscles, it is a natural tranquilizer. Dr. Mann says that since yogurt speeds up digestion, one carton in the evening helps combat sleeplessness and added, it also helps prevent intestinal side effects caused by antibiotics. Dr. Mann also said many pediatricians prescribe yogurt for babies whose stomachs cannot tolerate milk.

Yogurt and Intestinal Problems

Studies of yogurt have shown that intestinal ailments like constipation, diarrhea, indigestion and queasiness can be alleviated and even prevented by eating yogurt.

Research undertaken by three American scientists has demonstrated that yogurt killed 18 types of harmful bacteria, including those that cause dysentery and pneumonia.

One of the virtues of yogurt is that it is a 'live' food. On their way through their system, the bacteria do their healthful handiwork in your large intestine. (Yogurt will also do for your pets what it will do for you).

Yogurt and Antibiotics

Yogurt has been shown to combat positively the adverse effects of antibiotics on the system. Such drugs as penicillin, streptomycin, aureomycin and tetracycline destroy harmful bacterial that can cause infection, but also kill beneficial bacteria in the intestine. By eating yogurt with each meal, a person can restore their missing beneficial microorganisms within 36 to 48 hours.

Yogurt and Children

Babies and young children often have problems with diarrhea and digesting some foods. Yogurt was found to be more effective in treating children's diarrhea than some commercial products. Of course, if your child or infant is ill, you should contact your family physician.

Yogurt and People who Can't Drink Milk

People who suffer from lactose intolerance often turn to yogurt to get the protein and calcium nutrients their bodies require. In extreme cases of lactose intolerance, even yogurt may not be digested comfortably.

Yogurt and Seniors

Yogurt is especially good for the elderly who develop digestive disorders because of a lack of hydrochloric acid, which aids in digestion of proteins and Vitamin C. Yogurt counteracts this deficiency and makes digestion more efficient. It also has been shown to be effective in combating constipation and irregularity.

Yogurt and Longevity

Yogurt has long been linked to longevity. Those yogurt consuming people, who have past the century mark with as much energy as a teenager, lend credence to this claim. Unfortunately, yogurt has never been scientifically proven to promote longevity. Because of its beneficial effect on the large intestine, yogurt does help retard putrefaction, which is what occurs in the process of aging, yogurt can be said to stave off aging and thus help you live longer. This is true of course, provided you take care in other facets of your diet and health regime.

Yogurt and Weight

The key to dieting with yogurt is substitution. Yogurt is more nutritious and less fattening than most of the things we snack on and yet makes you feel full and satisfied. Yogurt can help you establish good eating habits – an important step in helping you reach and maintain your ideal weight. For your convenience, Olympic Dairy Products Ltd. produces Skim Milk and 2% Yogurt.

Yogurt may not be the "Fountain of Youth" so many are searching for, but it will make the years more enjoyable because it contributes to better health. It may not be the magic, all purpose healer but there are many ailments that it can either cure or alleviate.

Eating yogurt will undoubtedly make you feel better longer and isn't that what it's all about!

Main source of information The Yogurt Book, written by Connie Berman and Susan Katz, published by Gosset Dunlap.

COLORED ILLUSTRATIONS

APPETIZERS, DIPS & SAUCES

Nacho Appetizer

The Mexicans give up their Siesta for this snack!

1/2 lb.	**soft cream cheese**	**250 g**
1/2 cup	**Olympic Natural Yogurt**	**125 mL**
1 can	**hot Chili Con Carne**	**425 g**
1 cup	**Cheddar cheese, grated**	**250 g**

Mix cream cheese and yogurt together and spread on deep plate. Layer with chili and sprinkle Cheddar on top. Zap in microwave several minutes or until cheese is melted. Serve with Nachos or Tortillas.

Serves more men than women as the men can eat this a lot faster!

Petite Cordon Bleu Rolls

Perfect hors d'oeuvre for happy hour!

1-1/2 cups	**flour**	**375 mL**
1/2 cup	**butter, chilled**	**125 mL**
1/2 cup	**Olympic Natural Yogurt**	**125 mL**
18 slices	**chicken, cooked**	**18 slices**
9 slices	**cooked ham**	**9 slices**
1/2 lb.	**Swiss cheese**	**250 g**
1	**egg yolk**	**1**
3 tbsp.	**milk**	**45 mL**

Rub flour and butter into a fine meal using your fingers. Add yogurt and shape into a ball. Cover and chill for at least 8 hours. Cut each ham slice into two and cut cheese into 18 fingers. Roll cheese slices inside the ham slices so that the cheese doesn't melt out of the ends. Place on chicken slices and roll up tightly. Secure each roll with a toothpick. Roll out pastry to 1/8" thickness. Cut rectangles just large enough to wrap meat rolls in and remove toothpicks from rolls. Place the rolls on the dough and wrap up, overlapping to seal and crimp the ends with a fork. Place sealed side down on cookie sheet and score lightly. Mix egg yolk and milk together, whisking until blended. Glaze with egg wash and chill 1/2 hour or more before baking. Bake at 400° F. (200°C) for 20 to 25 minutes or until lightly browned.

Devilled Eggs

Attractive as well as good!

6	eggs, hard boiled	6
3 tbsp.	Olympic Natural Yogurt	45 mL
2 tbsp.	mayonnaise	30 mL
1 tsp.	chives, finely chopped	5 mL
1/2 tsp.	anchovy paste	2 mL
1 tsp.	powdered mustard	5 mL
	nutmeg	

Cut eggs in half lengthwise. In bowl mix egg yolks, yogurt, mayonnaise, chives, anchovy paste and mustard. When thoroughly mixed, fill egg halves with mixture and dust with nutmeg.

Marbled Curried Eggs

Stirring the eggs before they boil will centralize the egg yolks!

10	eggs	10
1/2 cup	tumeric	125 mL
2 tbsp.	Olympic Natural Yogurt	30 mL
1 tsp.	curry powder	5 mL
	paprika	

Place eggs in cold water. Cook over high heat until water boils. Reduce heat and boil gently, uncovered for 8 minutes. Drain. Lightly crack egg shells all over with a teaspoon but do not remove the shells. Place enough water in the same pan to cover the eggs when they are added later. Stir in tumeric and bring to a boil. Add eggs and simmer 5 minutes. Drain eggs and cover in cold water. Cool and remove shells. Cut in half and remove yolks. Combine yolks, yogurt and curry powder and mix well. Spoon mixture into egg whites and sprinkle with paprika. Makes 20 appetizers.

Try Olympic Natural Yogurt mixed with hard boiled eggs for an egg salad sandwich.

Eggplant Appetizer

No one would guess the base is eggplant!

1 lb.	**eggplant**	**500 g**
1 small	**onion, minced**	**1 small**
1 clove	**garlic, minced**	**1 clove**
1 tbsp.	**dill, finely chopped**	**15 mL**
1 tsp.	**lemon juice**	**5 mL**
1 cup	**Olympic Natural Yogurt**	**250 mL**
	salt and pepper	
3 tbsp.	**olive oil**	**45 mL**
1 large	**onion, sliced thin**	**1 large**

Bake eggplant on a sheet of foil for 1 hour or until inside is soft and skin has collapsed. Cool. Scrape out insides into a large bowl and mash or beat with a mixer. Add minced onion, garlic, dill, lemon juice and yogurt and blend well. Add salt and pepper and press into a pan and chill thoroughly. Meanwhile, saute onion slices in olive oil until lightly browned. Spoon on top of chilled mixture and serve with crackers.

Marinated Mushrooms

Choose fresh, tightly closed mushrooms for best results!

1 lb.	**button mushrooms**	**500 g**
1 cup	**Olympic Natural Yogurt**	**250 mL**
2 tbsp.	**olive oil**	**30 mL**
1 tbsp.	**lemon juice**	**15 mL**
	salt and pepper	

Gently brush mushrooms with a mushroom brush or wipe with a clean cloth and cut off the stems level with the base of each cap. (Reserve the stems for soup). Combine remaining ingredients and mix well. Add the mushrooms and mix until they are completely covered with the marinade. Cover and refrigerate at least 2 hours before serving. Serve with toothpicks.

Hot Mushroom Turnovers

These freeze well so keep a supply on hand for unexpected guests!

Dough

1/2 lb.	cream cheese	250 g
1/2 cup	butter	125 mL
1-1/2 cups	flour	375 mL

Soften cream cheese and butter. Work in flour and mix until it forms a soft ball. Wrap dough in waxed paper and refrigerate 1 hour.

Filling

1/2 lb.	mushrooms, chopped fine	250 g
1 large	onion, minced	1 large
3 tbsp.	olive oil	45 mL
1/4 tsp.	thyme	1 mL
2 tbsp.	flour	30 mL
1/4 cup	Olympic Natural Yogurt	50 mL
1 tsp.	salt	5 mL
1	egg, beaten	1

Fry mushrooms and onion in oil for about 5 minutes. Stir in dry ingredients and blend until smooth. Add yogurt and salt to mixture. Roll dough thinly on lightly floured board. Cut into 3" circles. Brush edges of circles with beaten egg. Place a spoonful of mushroom mix on half of circle. Fold over and crimp edges with a fork. make air holes in top with fork. Brush tops with beaten egg. Bake on ungreased cookie sheet at 350° F. (180°C) for 12 to 15 minutes. Serve hot.

Add caviar to Olympic Natural Yogurt for an exquisite dip!

Hummus

A traditional Greek dish served with toasted pita triangles!

19 oz.	can garbanzo beans (chick peas) drained	540 mL
1/4 cup	tahini (sesame paste)	60 mL
1/2 tsp.	cumin	2 mL
1/2 tsp.	salt	2 mL
	pepper	
3 cloves	garlic	3 cloves
2 tbsp.	lemon juice	30 mL
1/2 cup	Olympic Natural Yogurt	125 mL
	fresh parsley, chopped	
	pita bread, toasted or fried	

Combine all ingredients, except parsley and pita bread, in a blender or food processor and mix well. Add some liquid from the beans, if required. Sprinkle the parsley over the hummus and serve with pita bread.

Tzatziki

A natural combination with Pita Bread!

1	English cucumber, chopped	1
1 tsp.	salt	5 mL
2 cups	Olympic Natural Yogurt	500 mL
3 cloves	garlic, crushed	3 cloves
1 tbsp.	olive oil	15 mL
1 tsp.	lemon juice	5 mL
1 tsp.	wine vinegar	5 mL
1 tsp.	dill weed	5 mL
	lemon pepper	

Sprinkle cucumber with salt and let drain for 1/2 hour. Squeeze out excess moisture and combine with the rest of ingredients. Refrigerate overnight.

Salmon Spread with Capers

Use to stuff vegetables, such as snow peas, or cherry tomatoes or serve as a spread with pita bread or crackers!

7-1/2 oz.	tin sockeye salmon	213 g
1/4 cup	capers	60 mL
1/3 cup	celery, finely chopped	75 mL
2 tbsp.	Olympic Natural Yogurt	30 mL
1 tsp.	lemon juice	5 mL
	Tabasco sauce	
2 tbsp.	fresh parsley, chopped	30 mL

Flake salmon, along with juices and add capers, celery, yogurt and lemon juice. Add Tabasco to taste and sprinkle with parsley if using as a spread.

Walnut Sauce

Good with seafood, fish or poultry salads!

1/4 cup	Olympic Natural Yogurt	60 mL
2 tbsp.	lemon juice	30 mL
2 cloves	garlic, minced	2 cloves
2 tbsp.	walnuts, chopped	30 mL
1 tbsp.	fresh basil	15 mL
	salt and pepper	

Beat the yogurt with a whisk until it forms stiff peaks. Add the lemon juice. Fold in the remaining ingredients and refrigerate for several hours. Beat again just before serving. Makes about 1-1/2 cups.

Heat Olympic Natural Yogurt with Cheddar or Swiss cheese for a zesty cheese sauce!

Yogurt Hollandaise

Can be made ahead and reheated!

3/4 cup	Olympic Natural Yogurt	185 mL
2 tsp.	lemon (or lime) juice	10 mL
3	egg yolks	3
1 tsp.	Dijon mustard	5 mL
1/4 tsp.	salt	1 mL
pinch	pepper	pinch
dash	Tabasco sauce	dash

In top of double boiler, whisk together yogurt, lemon juice, egg yolks, mustard, salt, pepper and Tabasco sauce. Cook over simmering water, stirring constantly for 8 to 12 minutes or until sauce is thick. Taste and adjust seasoning.

Bernaise Sauce

The classic accompaniment to steak!

4	egg yolks, beaten	4
1 cup	Olympic natural Yogurt	250 mL
1/4 cup	white wine	60 mL
1/4 cup	vinegar	60 mL
1 tbsp.	shallots, minced	15 mL
1 clove	garlic, crushed	1 clove
1 tsp.	tarragon	5 mL
1 tsp.	chervil	5 mL
	salt	
	cayenne	
	freshly ground pepper	

Combine wine, vinegar, shallots, garlic, tarragon and chervil in a saucepan and bring to a boil, reducing liquid to practically a glaze. Combine glaze and egg yolks in the top of a double boiler. Using a whisk, beat in yogurt, a little at a time. Continue cooking and beating until sauce thickens. Do not let water boil. Add salt, cayenne and pepper. Makes about 1-3/4 cups.

Celebration Sauce

Serve with cold meat, fish platters or salad!

2 cups	mushrooms, sliced	500 mL
2 tbsp.	lemon juice	30 mL
3	green onions, sliced	3
1 tbsp.	vinegar	15 mL
1/2 tsp.	sugar	2 mL
	salt and pepper	
1 tbsp.	prepared mustard	15 mL
dash	Tabasco sauce	dash
1 cup	Olympic Natural Yogurt	250 mL

In a skillet, combine mushrooms and lemon juice and cook about 5 minutes. Place mushrooms and liquid in a bowl, cover and chill. Blanch green onions by pouring boiling water over them and draining immediately. Cover with cold water and drain again. Mix vinegar, sugar, salt and pepper together and pour over the onions. Cover and chill. At serving time, blend mustard, Tabasco and yogurt together. Drain the mushrooms and add to the yogurt mixture, along with the onions. Mix well and serve.

Spicy Coriander and Mint Chutney

Excellent served with Loin of Lamb!

1 cup	fresh coriander, chopped	250 mL
1/3 cup	fresh mint leaves, chopped	75 mL
1 tbsp.	jalapeno pepper, chopped	15 mL
1/2 tsp.	garlic, minced	2 mL
1 tsp.	fresh ginger, minced	5 mL
2 tbsp.	lemon juice	30 mL
1/4 tsp.	cumin	1 mL
1 tsp.	honey or sugar	5 mL
	salt and pepper	
1/4 cup	Olympic Natural Yogurt	60 mL

Puree the coriander, mint, jalapeno pepper, garlic, ginger, lemon juice, cumin, honey, salt and pepper. Whisk in the yogurt. Make up to 3 hours ahead and chill. Makes 3/4 cup.

Yogurt Dill Sauce

Good with turkey burger or with salmon!

1/2 cup	Olympic Natural Yogurt	125 mL
2 tbsp.	mayonnaise	30 mL
1 tsp.	dill weed	5 mL
1/2 tsp	Dijon mustard	2 mL
1 tsp.	prepared horseradish	5 mL
1/2 tsp.	lemon pepper	2 mL
dash	Tabasco sauce	dash
	salt	

Combine all ingredients and chill until needed. Makes about 1 cup (250 mL).

Coriander Yogurt Sauce

Makes a nice relish for hamburgers!

1/2 cup	Olympic Natural Yogurt	125 mL
2 tbsp.	tomato, diced	30 mL
1 tbsp.	green onion, chopped	15 mL
1 tbsp.	fresh coriander, chopped	15 mL
1/2 tsp.	prepared horseradish	2 mL
1/2 tsp.	Dijon mustard	2 mL

Combine all ingredients and mix well. Makes about 3/4 cup (185 mL).

Mix Olympic Natural Yogurt with onion soup mix for a quick party dip!

Yogurt Remoulade

This sauce is low calorie, and quick to prepare! Try serving with salmon!

1/2 cup	Olympic Natural Yogurt	125 mL
2 tbsp.	sour cream	30 mL
2 tbsp.	dill pickle, chopped	30 mL
1 tbsp.	fresh parsley, minced	15 mL
1 tsp.	Dijon mustard	5 mL
1 tsp.	fresh tarragon, minced	5 mL

Combine all ingredients thoroughly and serve on the side with fish. Makes about 2/3 cup (150 mL).

Liptauer

Strain the yogurt to remove some of the moisture for this recipe!

1-1/2 cup	Olympic Natural Yogurt	375 mL
2 tsp.	caraway seeds	10 mL
1 tsp.	paprika	5 mL
1/4 tsp.	cayenne pepper	1 mL
	freshly ground black pepper	

Combine all ingredients and chill to allow flavors to develop.

Mushroom Dip

This doesn't need to be kept in the dark!

2 tbsp.	olive oil	30 mL
6	mushrooms finely chopped	6
2	scallions, finely chopped	2
1/2 cup	Olympic Natural Yogurt	125 mL
1/2 cup	sour cream	125 mL
1 clove	garlic, crushed	1 clove
1 tsp.	salt	5 mL
dash	pepper	dash
	parsley	

Saute the mushrooms and scallions in olive oil until golden brown. Cool. Cream the remaining ingredients together in a bowl except the parsley, blending until smooth. Add the sauteed mixture and adjust the seasonings. Refrigerate until well chilled. Garnish with parsley. Makes 2-1/2 cups.

Herbed Avocado Sauce

Good with vegetables or steamed fish!

2	ripe avocados, peeled and pitted	2
2 tbsp.	lemon juice	30 mL
2/3 cup	dry white wine	150 mL
1/2 cup	clam juice	125 mL
1 clove	garlic, minced	1 clove
1/4 cup	watercress, chopped	60 mL
1/4 cup	parsley, chopped	60 mL
2 tbsp.	fresh basil, chopped	30 mL
2 tbsp.	fresh chervil, chopped	30 mL
1 tbsp.	fresh tarragon, chopped	15 mL
3 tbsp.	Olympic Natural Yogurt	45 mL
	salt and pepper	
	Tabasco sauce	

Puree the avocado and add the lemon juice. In a saucepan, combine the wine, clam juice and garlic and bring to a boil. Stir in the watercress, parsley, basil, chervil and tarragon and boil for 3 to 4 minutes. Remove from heat. When cool, puree. Combine the two pureed mixtures and add the yogurt, salt, pepper and Tabasco sauce. Adjust seasoning and gently heat until warm. Makes 2 cups.

Mint Sauce

Excellent with lamb!

1 cup	Olympic Natural Yogurt	250 mL
1/3 cup	lemon juice	75 mL
1/4 cup	fresh mint, chopped	60 mL
	salt and pepper	

Beat all ingredients thoroughly and refrigerate, covered, for at least 2 hours to allow the flavors to mingle. Makes about 1-1/2 cups.

Add Olympic Natural Yogurt to basic white sauce for a tangy taste!

Curry and Green Onion Sauce

Serve with meat or vegetables!

1 cup	Olympic Natural Yogurt	250 mL
2 tbsp.	green onion, finely chopped	30 mL
2 tsp.	curry powder	10 mL
	salt to taste	

Combine all ingredients and blend well. Chill and serve.

Marmalade Sauce

Use your favorite jam!

2 tbsp.	jam or marmalade	30 mL
1 cup	Olympic Natural Yogurt	250 mL

Whip together and serve with fruit.

Walnut Ginger Sauce

This is a favorite with ginger lovers!

1/4 cup	candied ginger, finely chopped	60 mL
1/2 cup	walnuts, minced	125 mL
1 tbsp.	honey	15 mL
2 cups	Olympic Natural Yogurt	250 mL

Mix first three ingredients together and fold in yogurt. Serve with fruit or put a dollop on fruit salad.

Add a little sugar to Olympic Natural Yogurt for a quick sauce for fruit!

Hawaiian Spread

Kids love this stuffed in celery!

1 cup	Olympic Natural Yogurt	250 mL
1/2 cup	crushed pineapple	125 mL
1/4 cup	dates, finely chopped	60 mL
1/2 cup	coconut	125 mL

Mix well and chill. Serve with fruit.

Lemon Yogurt Sauce

Spoon over fresh fruit slices!

3/4 cup	Olympic Natural Yogurt	185 mL
2 tbsp.	sugar	30 mL
	grated zest of lemon	

Combine ingredients and serve. Keeps covered in refrigerator for several days. Makes about 3/4 cup (185 mL).

Maple Yogurt Sauce

Complements apple dishes nicely!

3/4 cup	Olympic Natural Yogurt	185 mL
1/4 cup	maple syrup	60 mL

Combine yogurt and maple syrup and serve over your favorite apple dish or serve with Pancakes (see Breakfast, Brunch & Beverage Section). Makes 1 cup (250 mL).

Combine Olympic Natural Yogurt, coffee and brandy for a quick dessert sauce!

Citrus Fruit Dip

A nice clean taste!

2	eggs	2
1/2 cup	sugar	125 mL
1/4 cup	lemon juice	60 mL
1/4 cup	orange juice	60 mL
3/4 cup	Olympic Natural Yogurt	185 mL

Beat eggs slightly, then add sugar, lemon juice and orange juice. Cook over medium heat, stirring constantly until mixture comes to a boil and thickens. Cover with plastic wrap and cool. Fold in yogurt and chill well. Makes an excellent fruit dip. Yield is approximately 2 cups (500 mL).

Tropical Dip

Another excellent fruit dip!

2 tbsp.	frozen orange juice concentrate	30 mL
2 tsp.	liquid honey	10 mL
1	banana	1
2/3 cup	Olympic Natural Yogurt	150 mL

Blend orange juice concentrate, honey and banana at medium speed until smooth. Fold in yogurt. Cover and refrigerate for several hours. Serve with fruit.

Fruit Dip

Use any selection of fresh fruits!

1 cup	whipping cream	250 mL
1/3 cup	icing sugar	75 mL
1 tsp.	almond extract	5 mL
1 cup	Olympic Natural Yogurt	250 mL

Whip cream until it forms peaks. Add icing sugar and almond extract and beat until stiff. Fold in yogurt. Refrigerate.

Substitute Olympic Natural Yogurt for sour cream and/or mayonnaise in your favorite dip!

Herb Garden Dip

Herb's friends love it too!

1/2 cup	mayonnaise	125 mL
1/2 cup	Olympic Natural Yogurt	125 mL
1 tbsp.	lemon juice	15 mL
2 tbsp.	carrot, grated	30 mL
1 tbsp.	green onion, finely chopped	15 mL
1 tbsp.	fresh parsley, chopped	15 mL
1-1/2 tsp.	dill weed	7 mL
1 tsp.	sugar	5 mL
	dash pepper	
	salt	
2 tsp.	Dijon mustard	10 mL

Blend mayonnaise, yogurt and lemon juice until smooth. Stir in carrot, onion, parsley, dill, sugar, pepper, salt and Dijon. Cover and refrigerate several hours to meld flavors. Serve with crackers or fresh veggies.

Curried Shrimp Dip

This one got top honours in a taste test!

1/2 cup	Olympic Natural Yogurt	125 mL
1/2 cup	sour cream	125 mL
1/2 cup	mayonnaise	125 mL
1/4 cup	fresh shrimp	60 mL
1/4 cup	onion, finely chopped	60 mL
1 clove	garlic, minced	1 clove
1 tbsp.	curry powder	15 mL
1 tsp.	cumin	5 mL
	Tabasco sauce	
	salt	
	pepper	

Blend yogurt, sour cream and mayonnaise until smooth. Blend in remaining ingredients adjusting seasoning to taste. Chill to blend flavors. Serve with veggies.

Garlic Dip

Also a good fondue dip!

2 tbsp.	capers	30 mL
1-1/2 cups	Olympic Natural Yogurt	375 mL
1/4 cup	green onions, chopped	60 mL
4 cloves	garlic	4 cloves
1 tbsp.	olive oil	15 mL
1/2 tsp.	sugar	2 mL

Combine all ingredients in a bowl and mix thoroughly. Cover and refrigerate. Serve as a dip with chips or vegetables.

Mexican Spread

Add jalapenos if you prefer it really hot!

1 tsp.	chili powder	5 mL
1 cup	Olympic Natural Yogurt	250 mL
2 tsp.	onion, finely chopped	10 mL
2 oz.	jar pimentos, drained and chopped	60 mL
1/4 cup	black or green olives, sliced	60 mL
1 tsp.	hot dog relish	5 mL

Mix all ingredients thoroughly. Use as a dip for tacos or veggies.

Add your favorite fresh garden herbs to Olympic Natural Yogurt for a cool, refreshing veggie dip!

Cheddar Dip

Good with potato chips!

1 cup	**Cheddar cheese, grated**	**250 mL**
1/2 cup	**mayonnaise**	**125 mL**
1/2 cup	**Olympic Natural Yogurt**	**125 mL**
1/4 tsp.	**Tabasco Sauce**	**1 mL**

Mix all ingredients together and refrigerate for at least 1 hour. Yield 1-1/2 cups.

Salmon Dip

Serve as a dip or spoon into mushroom caps or cherry tomatoes.

7-1/2 oz.	**tin salmon, drained**	**213 g**
2 tbsp.	**Olympic Natural Yogurt**	**30 mL**
2 tbsp.	**sour cream**	**30 mL**
2 tbsp.	**mayonnaise**	**30 mL**
2 tsp.	**lemon juice**	**10 mL**
1/4 tsp.	**Worcestershire sauce**	**1 mL**
dash	**Tabasco sauce**	**dash**
	cilantro	

In food processor, process salmon until smooth. Add remainder of ingredients and process for 30 seconds.

Hot Mustard Dip

Serve with roast beef!

1 tbsp.	**hot mustard powder**	**15 mL**
1 tbsp.	**water**	**15 mL**
1/3 cup	**Olympic Natural Yogurt**	**75 mL**
1/3 cup	**mayonnaise**	**75 mL**
1 tbsp.	**chives, snipped**	**15 mL**

Mix mustard and water together. When smooth combine the balance of ingredients and add to mustard mixture. Mix thoroughly. Makes 1-1/2 cups.

BREAD, BISCUITS & MUFFINS

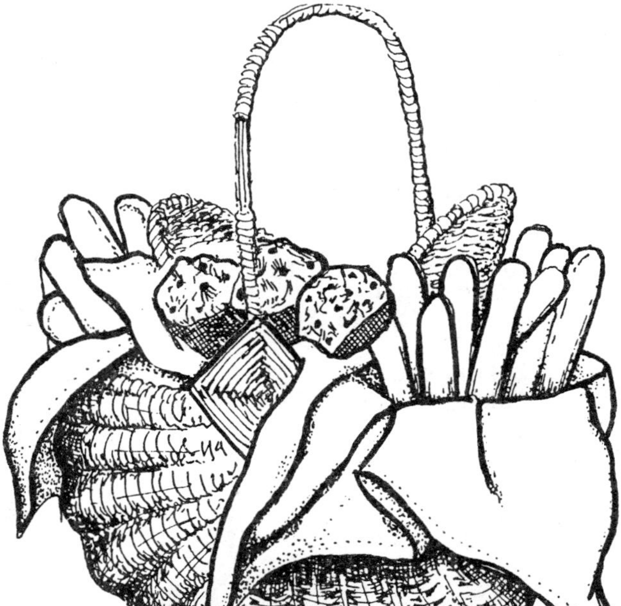

Refrigerator Bran Muffins

This batter keeps for up to six weeks in fridge!

2 cups	raisins	500 mL
2 cups	All Bran	500 mL
2 cups	boiling water	500 mL
3 cups	white sugar	750 mL
	OR	
1-1/2 cups	honey	375 mL
1 cup	oil	250 mL
4	eggs	4
5 cups	flour	1.2 L
1 tsp.	salt	5 mL
3 tbsp.	baking soda	45 mL
4 cups	Bran Buds	1 L
2 cups	Olympic Natural Yogurt	500 mL
1 cup	pecans, walnuts or sunflower seeds	250 mL

Mix raisins, All Bran and boiling water together and cool. Add rest of ingredients, mix well and drop into muffin tins. Bake at 375° F. (190°C) for 20 minutes or until firm. Cool on racks. Makes 4 dozen.

Rhubarb Muffins

Make lots of these in May when the rhubarb is fresh!

1 cup	rolled oats	250 mL
1/2 cup	brown sugar	125 mL
1 cup	Olympic Natural Yogurt	250 mL
1 cup	flour	250 mL
1/2 tsp.	baking soda	2 mL
2 tsp.	baking powder	10 mL
pinch	salt	pinch
1/2 tsp.	cinnamon	2 mL
1	egg, beaten	1
1/3 cup	oil	75 mL
2/3 cup	rhubarb, chopped very fine	150 mL

Combine oats, sugar and yogurt. Let stand 10 minutes. Mix flour, soda, baking powder, salt and cinnamon and set aside. To oat mixture, add egg and oil then add this mixture to dry ingredients stirring just enough to moisten. Fill greased muffin tins half full, add rhubarb, then top with more batter. Bake at 375° F. (190°C) for 20 minutes. Makes 1 dozen.

Note: Use up your leftover cranberry sauce along with grated orange zest in place of rhubarb. Or substitute 1 cup (250 mL) applesauce along with 1/2 cup (125 mL) raisins.

Orange and Pecan Bran Muffins

And good for you too!

2 cups	bran	500 mL
1 cup	flour	250 mL
1/4 cup	wheat germ	60 mL
2 tsp.	baking soda	10 mL
1/2 tsp.	salt	2 mL
1 cup	dates, chopped	250 mL
1/2 cup	pecans, chopped	125 mL
1 tbsp.	grated orange zest	15 mL
1/3 cup	melted butter or oil	75 mL
1/3 cup	molasses or corn syrup	75 mL
1-1/3 cups	Olympic Natural Yogurt	325 mL

Combine bran, flour, wheat germ, soda and salt. Add chopped dates, pecans and orange zest and toss lightly to separate and coat the dates. Combine butter, molasses and yogurt. Pour over dry ingredients and stir together just until blended. Pour into large greased or paper lined muffin tins, filling each to the top. Bake at 400° F. (200°C) 20 to 25 minutes or until well risen and firm to the touch. Yield is 12 large muffins.

Note: Try different variations of fruits/citrus fruits/nuts and create your very own recipe!

Cheddar Cheese Muffins

Moist and cheesy!

2 cups	all purpose flour	500 mL
1/2 cup	sugar	125 mL
1 tbsp.	baking powder	15 mL
1/2 tsp.	salt	2 mL
1/2 tsp.	baking soda	2 mL
2 cups	Cheddar cheese, grated	250 g
1 cup	Olympic Natural Yogurt	250 mL
1/4 cup	melted butter	60 mL
2	eggs, beaten	2

Blend together flour, sugar, baking powder, salt and baking soda. Gradually add cheese until evenly mixed and make a well. Whisk yogurt, butter and eggs together and pour into well. Stir until evenly moistened. Batter will be very thick. Spoon into greased muffin tins. Bake in center of oven for 18 to 20 minutes at 400° F. (200°C) or until golden. If you happen to have any left, they freeze well. Makes 12 muffins.

Note: Try adding 1 tbsp. dill weed for a unique taste! Or 1/2 cup cooked ham!

Blueberry Muffins

Colorful and yummy!

2 cups	whole wheat flour	500 mL
1 tsp.	baking soda	5 mL
1 tsp.	baking powder	5 mL
1/4 tsp.	salt	1 mL
1 cup	blueberries, fresh or frozen	250 mL
1	egg, well beaten	1
1 cup	brown sugar, packed	250 mL
1/4 cup	butter, melted	60 mL
1/2 tsp.	vanilla	2 mL
1 cup	Olympic Natural Yogurt	250 mL

Combine flour, baking soda, baking powder and salt, add blueberries and mix well. Make a well in the center. Beat egg with brown sugar and melted butter. Add vanilla and yogurt and beat well. Pour into well in dry ingredients and stir just until mixed. Fill greased muffin tins level with top of pan. Bake at 400°F. (200°C) for 20 minutes. Let cool for five minutes before removing to a rack to finish cooling. Makes 12.

Note: Try 1 cup (250 mL) mashed banana along with 1/2 cup (125 mL) chopped dates for a variation in place of blueberries.

Banana Oatmeal Muffins

What a great way to start the day!

1 cup	flour	250 mL
1/2 cup	brown sugar	125 mL
1 tsp.	baking powder	5 mL
1/2 tsp.	salt	2 mL
1/2 tsp.	baking soda	2 mL
1 cup	rolled oats	250 mL
1	banana, mashed	1
1	egg	1
3/4 cup	Olympic Natural Yogurt	185 mL
1/3 cup	shortening, melted	75 mL

Mix flour, sugar, baking powder, salt, baking soda and rolled oats. Combine banana, egg, yogurt and shortening and add to dry ingredients stirring as little as possible. Fill greased muffin tins 2/3 full and bake 15 minutes at 400° F. (200°C). Makes 12 muffins.

Pineapple Yogurt Muffins

Chunky bits of pineapple, enhanced by the taste of orange, make these special!

1-1/2 cups	whole wheat flour	375 mL
1/2 cup	oat bran	125 mL
1 tsp.	baking powder	5 mL
1/2 tsp.	baking soda	2 mL
1-1/2 tsp.	cinnamon	7 mL
1/4 tsp.	nutmeg	1 mL
1/3 cup	brown sugar, firmly packed	75 mL
1 cup	Olympic Natural Yogurt	250 mL
1/4 cup	water	60 mL
2 tbsp.	oil	30 mL
2	egg whites	2
1-1/2 tsp.	vanilla	7 mL
1 tsp.	grated orange zest	5 mL
1 cup	crushed pineapple, drained	250 mL

Combine flour, oat bran, baking powder, baking soda and spices. Mix well. In another bowl combine brown sugar, yogurt, water, oil, egg whites, vanilla and orange zest. Beat with a whisk until blended. Stir in pineapple and add to dry mixture. Mix until all ingredients are moistened. Pour into greased muffin tins and bake 18 to 20 minutes at 375° F. (190°C) until toothpick inserted into the center of the muffin comes out clean. Remove muffins to a rack to cool.
Makes 10.

Experiment with your favorite recipes!

Red Pepper Muffins

Perfect for breakfast or snacks and very attractive!

1 cup	red bell pepper, finely chopped	250 mL
2 tbsp.	butter	30 mL
1 cup	unbleached white flour	250 mL
1/2 tsp.	salt	2 mL
1-1/2 tsp.	baking soda	7 mL
1/2 tsp.	baking powder	2 mL
1/4 cup	brown sugar, packed	60 mL
1-1/4 cups	corn meal	300 mL
1	egg	1
1 cup	Olympic Natural Yogurt	250 mL

Saute the pepper in butter over low heat until soft, about 10 minutes and set aside. Sift together flour, salt, baking soda, and baking powder. Stir in brown sugar and corn meal and mix thoroughly. Beat egg and yogurt and stir into flour mixture along with the pepper. Spoon batter into greased muffin tins, filling until even with the top of the pan. Bake at 400° F. (200°C) for 15 or 20 minutes, or until a toothpick inserted in the center comes out clean and tops are beginning to brown. Cool in the pan for about 10 minutes before removing.
Yields one dozen muffins.

RaspberryCorn Muffins

Experiment with other kinds of berries as well!

1 cup	corn meal	250 mL
1 cup	unbleached white flour	250 mL
1/2 tsp.	salt	2 mL
1/2 cup	brown sugar, packed	125 mL
1 tsp.	baking powder	5 mL
1/2 tsp.	baking soda	2 mL
1	large egg	1
1/4 cup	butter, melted	60 mL
1/2 cup	Olympic Natural Yogurt	125 mL
1/2 cup	orange juice	125 mL
1/4 tsp.	grated orange zest	1 mL
1 cup	raspberries, fresh (or frozen thawed and drained)	250 mL

Combine corn meal, flour, salt, sugar, baking powder and baking soda and make a well. Combine the egg, butter. yogurt and orange juice and beat well. Pour into the well mixing until partially blended. Add the orange zest and the berries and continue to mix sparingly, just until completely moistened. Pour into greased muffin tins and bake for 15 to 20 minutes (depending on the size of the muffins) at 400° F. (200°C). Cool in the pan for 10 minutes before removing. Makes 6 large or 12 small muffins.

Oatmeal Carrot Muffins

Try making these "tart sized" for your kids!

1 cup	Olympic Natural Yogurt	250 mL
1 cup	quick cooking rolled oats	250 mL
1/2 cup	carrots, grated	125 mL
1/4 cup	brown sugar	60 mL
1/4 cup	butter, melted	60 mL
1	egg, slightly beaten	1
1 tsp.	grated orange zest	5 mL
1 cup	all purpose flour	250 mL
1/4 cup	granulated sugar	60 mL
1 tbsp.	baking powder	15 mL
1 tsp.	salt	5 mL
1/2 tsp.	baking soda	2 mL
3/4 cup	raisins	185 mL

Mix yogurt and oats together, cover and let stand two hours or overnight in the refrigerator. Mix carrots, brown sugar, butter, egg and orange zest together and stir into oat mixture. Sift together flour, sugar, baking powder, salt and baking soda. Stir in raisins. Mix batter just until moistened. Spoon into greased muffin tins, filling to the top. Bake at 400° F. (200°C) for 20 to 25 minutes. Let stand a few minutes before removing from tin. Makes 12 muffins.

Note: Try adding 1 tsp. of a herb such as basil, oregano or tarragon if you are a licorice fan!

Cheese Currant Soda Bread

Slice and serve!

2 cups	all purpose flour	500 mL
2 tbsp.	sugar	30 mL
1-1/2 tsp.	baking powder	7 mL
3/4 tsp.	salt	4 mL
1/2 tsp.	baking soda	2 mL
2 tbsp.	butter	30 mL
1 tsp.	caraway seeds	5 mL
1/4 cup	Cheddar cheese, grated	60 mL
1/4 cup	currants	60 mL
1	egg, beaten	1
1 cup	Olympic Natural Yogurt	250 mL

Combine flour, sugar, baking powder, salt and baking soda. Cut in butter. Add caraway seeds, cheese and currants. Mix egg and yogurt and add to dry ingredients, kneading lightly. Shape into a round loaf. Cut a cross on top about 1/4" deep and bake at 350° F. (180°C) for one hour. Makes one round loaf.

Pumpkin Nut Bread

Put this on your menu after carving the pumpkin!

1-1/2 cups	flour	375 mL
1-1/4 tsp.	baking soda	6 mL
1 tsp.	salt	5 mL
1 tsp.	cinnamon	5 mL
1/2 tsp.	nutmeg	2 mL
1 cup	pumpkin OR use canned pumpkin	250 mL
1 cup	sugar	250 mL
1/2 cup	Olympic Natural Yogurt	125 mL
1	egg	1
2 tbsp.	butter, softened	30 mL
1 cup	pecans, chopped	250 mL

Sift flour, soda, salt and spices together. Combine pumpkin, sugar, yogurt and egg. Add dry ingredients and butter and beat until well blended. Stir in pecans. Spread in well greased loaf pan and bake at 375° F. (190°C) for 45 minutes or until toothpick inserted in center comes out clean and top is golden brown. Makes 1 loaf.

Twists

You'll twist and shout for more!

1 tsp.	sugar	5 mL
1 tbsp.	active dry yeast (1 envelope)	15 mL
1/4 cup	lukewarm water	60 mL
1 cup	butter	250 mL
4 cups	all purpose flour	1 L
1 tsp.	salt	5 mL
3/4 cup	Olympic Natural Yogurt	185 mL
2	eggs, well beaten	2
1 tsp.	vanilla	5 mL
1/2 tsp.	grated lemon zest	2 mL
1-3/4 cups	sugar	425 mL

Dissolve 1 tsp. (5 mL) sugar and yeast in lukewarm water. Cut butter into flour and salt with a pastry blender. Add dissolved yeast, yogurt, eggs, vanilla and lemon zest. Combine thoroughly, cover with a damp cloth and refrigerate for two hours or overnight. Roll out half the dough on a well-sugared board. Fold ends toward center and sprinkle with 1 tbsp. (15 mL) sugar. Repeat rolling and sprinkling twice. Roll about 1/4" strip. Twist ends in opposite directions, stretching dough slightly. Place in shape of horseshoes on greased cookie sheets. Bake at 400° F. (200°C) for approximately 15 minutes. Remove from cookie sheet immediately. Makes 5 dozen.

Biscuits

For excitement, brush with beaten egg and sprinkle with sesame seeds before baking!

4 cups	flour	1 L
2 tbsp.	baking powder	30 mL
1 tsp.	baking soda	5 mL
3/4 tsp.	salt	4 mL
1 tbsp.	sugar	15 mL
2/3 cup	butter, softened	150 mL
1-3/4 cups	Olympic Natural Yogurt	425 mL
1/4 cup	melted butter	60 mL

Combine flour, baking powder, soda, salt, sugar and butter into a coarse meal. Add yogurt and stir until moist. Turn dough onto floured board and knead 4 to 5 times. Roll out 1/2" thick. Cut with 2" cutter and brush with melted butter. Bake at 450° F. (230°C) for 12 minutes or until golden. Makes approx. 2 dozen.

Yogurt Bread

Your family will never let you buy bread again!

1-1/2 cups	**warm water**	**375 mL**
2 tbsp.	**active dry yeast (2 packages)**	**30 mL**
1 cup	**Olympic Natural Yogurt**	**250 mL**
1 tbsp.	**salt**	**15 mL**
5 cups	**flour**	**1.2 L**

Pour water into mixing bowl and sprinkle yeast on top. Allow to rest for 5 minutes. Stir to dissolve yeast. Add yogurt and salt. Stir in flour, a little at a time, and knead the dough in the bowl until it is no longer sticky. Remove to floured surface and knead until dough is stiff. Form into a ball and place in a lightly greased bowl and cover. Let rise in a warm place until doubled in bulk, approximately 1-1/2 hours. Punch dough down and cut into two pieces. Shape each into a long loaf. Place in loaf tins, cover and allow to rise again for another hour or until double in size. Brush loaves with water. Bake at 400° F. (200°C) for 45 minutes or until crusts are golden brown and loaves sound hollow when tapped. Yield is 2 loaves.

Note: Try experimenting with herbs for a fresh healthy taste. Add 1 tsp. of savory or dill or combine several herbs, depending on your favorites!

Prune and Orange Scones

A prune scone a day keeps the doctor away!

3 cups	**flour**	**750 mL**
1/2 cup	**sugar**	**125 mL**
4 tsp.	**baking powder**	**20 mL**
1/2 tsp.	**salt**	**2 mL**
1/2 cup	**butter**	**125 mL**
1 cup	**prunes, pitted and chopped**	**250 mL**
1	**egg**	**1**
1 cup	**Olympic Natural Yogurt**	**250 mL**
2 tsp.	**grated orange zest**	**10 mL**
1	**egg**	**1**
1 tbsp.	**milk**	**15 mL**

Mix flour, sugar, baking powder and salt. Using pastry blender, cut in butter until mixture resembles coarse meal. Dust prunes well with flour. Beat egg with yogurt and add orange zest. Add yogurt mixture and prunes to flour mixture and mix well. Turn dough on to floured surface and knead lightly five or six times, adding more flour as needed to keep dough from sticking. Divide dough into 18 equal portions. Shape each portion into a ball, then flatten into discs 1/2" (1.15 cm thick). Place apart on ungreased baking sheet and brush lightly with a mixture of 1 egg and 1 tbsp. milk. Bake at 375° F. (190°C) oven 20 minutes or until golden brown. Serve warm. Yield 18 scones.

(From left to right)

Yogurt Bread, page 36
Refrigerator Bran Muffins, page 28
Cheddar Cheese Muffins, page 29
Whole Wheat Zucchini Bread, page 41

Oat Scones

Serve warm!

1-3/4 cups	all purpose flour	425 mL
1/2 cup	rolled oats	125 mL
2 tbsp.	sugar	30 mL
1/2 tsp.	baking soda	2 mL
1/2 tsp.	salt	2 mL
1/4 cup	butter, chilled	60 mL
1/4 cup	shortening, chilled	60 mL
2	eggs	2
1/2 cup	Olympic Natural Yogurt	125 mL
1/4 tsp.	salt	1 mL
2 tbsp.	rolled oats	30 mL

Stir together flour, 1/2 cup (125 mL) rolled oats, sugar, baking soda and 1/2 tsp. (2 mL) salt. Cut in butter and shortening until mixture resembles coarse crumbs. Combine one of the eggs with the yogurt and stir into flour mixture to form dough. On floured board, knead gently into a ball. Pat into buttered 9" round cake pan. Cut into 8 wedges, cutting only partway through. Whisk together remaining egg and 1/4 tsp. (1 mL) salt and brush over scones. Sprinkle with 2 tbsp. (30 mL) rolled oats. Bake in 425° F. (220°C) oven for 15 to 20 minutes or until puffed and browned. Turn out onto wire rack. Yield 8 scones.

Lemon Yogurt Scones

In a crunch, fold in 1/2 cup (125 mL) chopped pecans!

2 cups	all purpose flour	500 mL
2 tbsp.	sugar	30 mL
1 tbsp.	baking powder	15 mL
1/2 tsp.	baking soda	2 mL
1/2 tsp.	salt	2 mL
1/2 cup	butter, chilled	125 mL
1 cup	Olympic Natural Yogurt	250 mL
1 tsp.	grated lemon zest	5 mL

Combine flour, sugar, baking powder, baking soda, salt and mix well. Cut in butter with pastry blender until mixture is crumbly. Add yogurt and lemon zest, stir until just moistened. Form into a ball, pat dough out on lightly floured surface to 1" (2.5 cm) thickness. Use 2" (5 cm) cookie cutter to cut out scones. Place on ungreased cookie sheet and bake in 425° F. (220°C) oven 12 to 14 minutes or until done. Makes one dozen.

Mock Sourdough Bread

Start making after lunch and it will be ready for an after school treat!

2 cups	Olympic Natural Yogurt	500 mL
1 tbsp.	active dry yeast (1 package)	15 mL
1/4 cup	warm water	60 mL
1 tbsp.	sugar	15 mL
2 tsp.	salt	10 mL
1 tbsp.	oil	15 mL
4 cups	all purpose flour	1 L
	cold water	

Heat yogurt to lukewarm. Dissolve yeast in warm water and stir in yogurt, sugar, salt, oil and 2 cups (500 mL) of the flour. Beat until smooth. Stir in enough remaining flour to make dough easy to handle. Turn dough onto lightly floured surface, knead until smooth and elastic, about 5 minutes. Place in greased bowl, turn greased side up, cover and let rise in warm place until double in size, about 1 hour. (Dough is ready if an indentation remains when touched). Punch dough down and divide into 8 equal parts. Shape into loaves and place on greased baking sheet. Brush tops lightly with cold water. With a sharp knife, cut 3 diagonal slashes across the top of each loaf. Let rise until doubled, about 25 minutes. Heat oven to 375° F. (190°C). Brush loaves with cold water. Bake until they sound hollow when tapped, 30 to 35 minutes, brushing with water twice during baking time. Cool on wire rack. Makes 8 individual loaves.

Whole Wheat Honey Bread

And it is good for them besides!

1/4 cup	warm water	60 mL
1 tsp.	honey	5 mL
1 tbsp.	active dry yeast (1 package)	15 mL
1 tsp.	salt	5 mL
1 cup	Olympic Natural Yogurt	250 mL
2 tbsp.	oil	30 mL
3 tbsp.	honey	45 mL
1 cup	whole wheat flour	250 mL
1 cup	all purpose flour	250 mL

Mix 1 tsp. (5 mL) honey with warm water and sprinkle yeast on top. Allow to dissolve for 10 minutes. Add salt, yogurt, oil and 3 tbsp. (45 mL) honey and mix well gradually adding flours alternately to form a soft dough. If required, add extra white flour. Knead well, cover and let rise for 1 hour or until doubled in size. Knead dough again and shape into a loaf. Place in pan, cover and let rise until doubled in volume. Bake at 375° F. (190°C) for 45 to 50 minutes or until loaf sounds hollow when tapped. Makes one large loaf.

Boston Brown Bread

They like this as far away as Ireland!

1/3 cup	sifted white flour	75 mL
1/3 tsp.	baking powder	3 mL
1/3 tsp.	baking soda	3 mL
1/3 tsp.	salt	3 mL
1/3 cup	yellow cornmeal	75 mL
1/3 cup	whole wheat flour	75 mL
1/3 cup	nuts, chopped	75 mL
1/4 cup	molasses	60 mL
2/3 cup	Olympic Natural Yogurt	150 mL
1/3 cup	raisins	75 mL

Sift white flour with baking powder, baking soda and salt. Stir in cornmeal and whole wheat flour. Add remaining ingredients and beat well. Bake in a small loaf pan for 1 hour at 300° F. (150°C). Makes one loaf.

Whole Wheat Zucchini Bread

This version is lower in fat and cholesterol than most!

1-1/2 cups	all purpose flour	375 mL
1-1/2 cups	whole wheat flour	375 mL
1 tbsp.	cinnamon	15 mL
1 tsp.	nutmeg	5 mL
1 tsp.	pumpkin pie spice	5 mL
1 tsp.	baking soda	5 mL
1 tsp.	baking powder	5 mL
1/2 tsp.	salt	2 mL
3/4 cup	raisins	185 mL
1 cup	walnuts, chopped	250 mL
2	eggs, beaten	2
1/3 cup	vegetable oil	75 mL
3/4 cup	Olympic Natural Yogurt	185 mL
1/4 cup	skim milk	60 mL
1 cup	brown sugar, packed	250 mL
2 tsp.	vanilla	10 mL
2 cups	zucchini, unpeeled, shredded	500 mL

Combine dry ingredients. To beaten eggs add oil, yogurt, milk, sugar and vanilla. Stir in zucchini. Add flour mixture and stir until combined. Pour batter into two well-greased loaf pans and bake at 350° F. (180°C) for 1 hour or until toothpick comes out clean. Remove from pan and let cool thoroughly before slicing. Makes 2 loaves.

Tandoori Bread

Fun to cook and fun to eat!

1 tbsp.	**active dry yeast (1 package)**	**15 mL**
3/4 cup	**warm water**	**185 mL**
1/2 tsp.	**salt**	**2 mL**
2-1/2 cups	**all purpose flour**	**625 mL**
1/4 cup	**oil**	**60 mL**
1 tbsp.	**Olympic Natural Yogurt**	**15 mL**

Soak yeast in water. Mix salt with flour and rub in the oil. Mix in yogurt and add the yeast mixture to form a dough. Cover and let rise about 5 hours. Punch down and knead well. Make into 12 rolls and roll each to crepe sized circles. Cook in ungreased heavy frying pan, turning to cook both sides evenly.

Indian Fried Bread

Give the job of frying this to one of your guests!

3 cups	**whole wheat flour**	**750 mL**
1 tsp.	**salt**	**5 mL**
1/2 cup	**butter**	**125 mL**
1-1/2 cups	**Olympic Natural Yogurt**	**375 mL**

Mix well and knead until smooth. Form balls, then roll into thin flat cakes. Fry in deep fat until puffed and brown. Serve at once.

Substitute Olympic Natural Yogurt for mayonnaise in sandwiches!

BREAKFAST, BRUNCH & BEVERAGES

Egyptian Eyes

You can also fry in the pan instead of baking in the oven!

4	slices bread	4
2 tbsp.	butter	30 mL
4	eggs	4
1/2 cup	Olympic Natural Yogurt	125 mL
	salt and pepper	
	minced parsley	

From the center of each piece of bread, cut out a small circle. (Freeze these circles and use when needed for bread crumbs). Saute the slices bread in butter and place them in a baking dish. Drop an egg into the center of each piece of bread, season and top with yogurt. Bake in 350° F. (180°C) until eggs are set, about 10 to 15 minutes. Sprinkle with parsley. Serves 2 to 4.

Ham and Eggs Au Gratin

For a change of pace, serve Ham and Eggs Au Gratin over pasta instead of toast!

1/4 cup	butter	60 mL
1/4 cup	flour	60 mL
1/2 tsp.	dry mustard powder	2 mL
1-1/2 cups	milk	375 mL
2 tsp.	Worcestershire sauce	10 mL
1 cup	Cheddar cheese, shredded	250 mL
1 cup	ham, cooked and cubed	250 mL
6	eggs, hard boiled and sliced	6
1/4 cup	Olympic Natural Yogurt	60 mL
6	slices toast	6

Melt butter and blend in flour and dry mustard. Stir in milk and cook until thickened. Add Worcestershire sauce and cheese and cook just until cheese melts. Mix in ham and eggs and cook until heated through. Remove from heat and fold in yogurt. Serve immediately over toast. Serves 4 to 6.

Eggs Benedict

These taste like you slaved for hours preparing them (and it only took you a few minutes)!

4	eggs	4
2	English muffins, toasted	2
4	slices ham, lightly fried	4
3/4 cup	Hollandaise sauce*	185 mL

Poach eggs. Split muffins and toast. Place each muffin on a serving plate, top with ham and poached egg. Pour Hollandaise sauce over eggs and serve at once.

Eggs Florentine (Eggs Nestled in Spinach)

You can serve the spinach in a large baking dish instead of individual dishes if desired!

I lb.	spinach, fresh	500 g
1 tsp.	butter	5 mL
	salt and pepper	
	nutmeg, freshly ground	
6	eggs, poached	6
3/4 cup	Hollandaise sauce*	185 mL

Cook spinach until it is wilted. Drain thoroughly and chop coarsely. Return to saucepan, add butter, salt, pepper and nutmeg. Divide evenly in ramekins making an indentation in the spinach (to form a nest). Place egg in "nest", top with Hollandaise Sauce and serve immediately.

*See following page.

Substitute Olympic Natural Yogurt for catsup with eggs.

*Yogurt Hollandaise Sauce

Can be made ahead and reheated!

3/4 cup	Olympic Natural Yogurt	185 mL
2 tsp.	lemon (or lime) juice	10 mL
3	egg yolks	3
1 tsp.	Dijon mustard	5 mL
1/4 tsp.	salt	1 mL
pinch	pepper	pinch
dash	Tabasco sauce	dash

In top of double boiler, whisk together yogurt, lemon juice, egg yolks, mustard, salt, pepper and hot pepper sauce. Cook over simmering water, stirring constantly for 8 to 12 minutes or until sauce is thick. Taste and adjust seasoning.

Brunch Bake

Enjoy a leisurely brunch that's easy to prepare!

	butter	
	Parmesan cheese, grated	
1	slice tomato, quartered	1
2 tbsp.	cooked chicken, chopped	30 mL
1	green onion, chopped	1
1/2	green pepper, chopped	1/2
	salt and pepper	
1/2 tsp.	basil (or tarragon)	2 mL
1	egg	1
1 tbsp.	Olympic Natural Yogurt	15 mL

Butter individual ramekin dishes and sprinkle with Parmesan cheese. Place tomato pieces, chicken, onion and green pepper in dish and sprinkle with salt, pepper and basil. Break egg over chicken mixture and spoon yogurt on top. Sprinkle with additional Parmesan cheese. Bake in oven at 350°F. (180°C) for 10 to 15 minutes or until egg is set. Serves 1.

French Toast

The yogurt gives a nice crunchy crust!

2	eggs, beaten with a fork	2
1 tsp.	vanilla	5 mL
1 tsp.	sugar	5 mL
pinch	salt	pinch
2 tbsp.	Olympic Natural Yogurt	30 mL
4	slices slightly stale bread	4
	butter	

Combine eggs, vanilla, sugar, salt and yogurt and whisk together. Dip bread slices in mixture and fry in butter in frying pan until both sides are browned. Serves 4.

Turkish Poached Eggs

A natural when only eggs and yogurt are left in the fridge!

1 cup	Olympic Natural Yogurt	250 mL
1	clove garlic, finely minced	1
1 tsp.	salt	5 mL
1 tbsp.	white wine vinegar	15 mL
4	eggs, poached	4
	pepper	
2 tbsp.	butter, melted	30 mL
dash	paprika	dash

Beat yogurt, garlic, salt and vinegar and pour into a serving dish or individual ramekins. Arrange poached eggs over the yogurt and sprinkle with pepper. Add paprika to the melted butter and pour over the eggs. Place in 375° F. (190°C) oven for about 10 minutes. Serves 4.

Omelette

Add bacon, tomatoes and/or peppers for a change!

3	eggs, lightly beaten	3
	salt	
	pepper	
1/3 cup	Olympic Natural Yogurt	75 mL
2 tbsp.	flour	30 mL
1 tbsp.	cold water	15 mL
dash	Tabasco Sauce	dash
dash	Worcestershire Sauce	dash
1/4 cup	Cheddar cheese, grated	60 mL
	butter for cooking in	

Add the salt and pepper to lightly beaten eggs. Mix the yogurt and flour together and whisk into eggs. Add the water, Tabasco, Worcestershire and pour half the mixture into a buttered frying pan. Cook over low heat until browned. Sprinkle over cheddar, fold in half and serve. Repeat with remaining batter. Serves 2.

Crustless Mushroom Quiche

Very easy and tasty!

1 tbsp.	butter	15 mL
6 slices	bacon, chopped	6 slices
1	onion, thinly sliced	1
12	mushrooms, sliced	12
1 cup	Swiss cheese, shredded	1/2 cup
4	eggs	4
1/2 cup	Olympic Natural Yogurt	125 mL
1/2 tsp.	dry mustard powder	2 mL
1/2 tsp.	nutmeg	2 mL
	salt and pepper	

Saute bacon in butter until cooked and drain on paper towel. Add onion and mushrooms to pan and cook lightly. When done spread evenly in the bottom of a greased quiche dish or pie plate, along with the bacon. Sprinkle the cheese over the mixture. Beat eggs lightly and add yogurt, mustard, nutmeg, salt and pepper and pour over cheese. Bake at 375° F. (190°C) for 20 minutes. Let stand 5 minutes to firm slightly before serving. Serves 4 to 6.

Brunch Crepes

Add whatever leftovers you have on hand (chicken, ham, etc.) to replace the seafood!

1/2 cup	flour	125 mL
1/4 tsp.	salt	1 mL
1	egg	1
1/2 cup	milk	125 mL
1/2 cup	Olympic Natural Yogurt	125 mL
1 tbsp.	olive oil	15 mL
2 tbsp.	brandy (optional)	30 mL
	butter for frying	

2 tbsp.	butter	30 mL
1/2 cup	mushrooms, sliced	125 mL
1/4 cup	green pepper, diced	60 mL
1/4 cup	celery, chopped	60 mL
1/4 cup	onion, chopped	60 mL
1/4 lb.	fresh crab meat	125 g.
1/4 lb.	fresh shrimp	125 g.
3 tbsp.	sherry	45 mL
3 tbsp.	flour	45 mL
1	egg yolk	1
1 cup	Olympic Natural Yogurt	250 mL

Crepes

Mix the flour and salt together, make a well and add the egg. Combine milk, yogurt, oil and brandy and mix. Add to the dry ingredients and whisk thoroughly to make a smooth batter. Refrigerate at least an hour to allow flour to expand and air bubbles to escape. To cook, follow the directions for a crepe maker or melt butter in a fry pan. Spoon some of the batter into the center of the pan and tilt so the batter runs to the edges of the pan, making a circle. Let cook until brown on the bottom, then flip over and brown the other side. If you are making the crepes ahead of time, stack between layers of waxed paper.

Filling

Melt butter and saute mushrooms until brown. Remove and add green pepper, celery and onion and fry until soft. Add to the mushrooms. Add crab meat and shrimp to the frying pan and sprinkle with sherry. Cook gently for 5 minutes. Add the flour and mix thoroughly. Beat the egg yolk and add to the yogurt. With the heat on low, blend the yogurt/egg mixture into the frying pan, along with the mushroom mixture and allow to thicken. Fill each crepe with a portion of the mixture and roll up. Spoon remaining filling over the crepes and reheat if necessary. Makes 4 to 6 crepes with filling.

Note: For a quick curried dish, add 1/2 tsp. curry powder, 1/2 tsp. dry mustard powder and 1 tsp. Worcestershire sauce to the yogurt/egg mixture.

Yogurt Pancakes

Nice crispy pancakes!

1 cup	Olympic Natural Yogurt	250 mL
2	egg yolks	2
1/4 cup	butter, melted	60 mL
3/4 cup	flour	185 mL
1 tbsp.	sugar	15 mL
1 tsp.	baking soda	5 mL
1/2 tsp.	salt	2 mL
2	egg whites beaten until stiff	2
	butter for frying	

1/2 cup	Olympic Natural Yogurt	125 mL
2 tbsp.	maple syrup	30 mL
2 cups	raspberries, blueberries, etc	250 mL

Combine yogurt, egg yolks and butter until well mixed. Add dry ingredients, then gently fold in beaten egg whites. Spoon the batter onto a greased griddle. When bubbles pop, turn and brown on the other side. Meanwhile, mix the yogurt and maple syrup. Top the pancakes with berries and spoon over the maple yogurt. Makes about 8 pancakes.

Out-the-Door-Breakfast

You can sleep in an extra half hour and still have your morning energy!

1 cup	Olympic Natural Yogurt	250 mL
2 tbsp.	wheat germ	30 mL
1	egg	1
2 tbsp.	brown sugar or honey	30 mL
2 tbsp.	frozen orange juice	30 mL
1	banana	1

Whirl all ingredients together in a blender until smooth. Chill before serving if possible. Makes 1 serving.

Lassi

A traditional Indian Yogurt Beverage!

1 cup	Olympic Natural Yogurt	250 mL
2 cups	water	500 mL
	OR	
	fruit juice (pineapple, apricot, etc.)	
dash	salt	dash
1/4 tsp.	nutmeg	1 mL
1 tbsp.	honey	15 mL
pinch	cayenne (to sharpen flavors)	pinch

Whirl in blender until smooth. Serve chilled. Serves 2.

Bleeding Mary

Substitute Clamato Juice for tomato juice if you prefer a Bleeding Caesar!

1/2 cup	Olympic Natural Yogurt	125 mL
1/2 cup	tomato juice	125 mL
	celery salt	
dash	Tabasco sauce	dash
	dilly bean	

Mix yogurt, juice, celery salt and Tabasco. Chill before serving. Add a dilly bean for garnish. Makes 1 glass.

Strawberry Cooler

Try any fruit in place of strawberries!

1 cup	strawberries, sliced	250 mL
1 cup	Olympic Natural Yogurt	250 mL
1 cup	milk	250 mL
2 tbsp.	honey	30 mL

Whip all ingredients in a blender until smooth. Makes 3 cups.

Chocolate Yogurt Brandy

Just for the adults!

1/2 cup	chocolate ice cream	125 mL
1 cup	Olympic Natural Yogurt	250 mL
2 tbsp.	brandy	30 mL
	whipped cream	
	cocoa	

Place ice cream, yogurt and brandy in blender and blend until smooth. Pour into tall glass. Garnish with whipped cream and a pinch of cocoa. Makes 1-1/2 cups.

Combine fresh fruit, Olympic Natural Yogurt and ice cubes in blender for a refreshing drink!

Red Eye

The Aussies must have thought this up!

1/3 cup	Olympic Natural Yogurt	75 mL
2/3 cup	beet juice	150 mL
pinch	dill weed	pinch

Blend together and serve in chilled glasses. Makes 1 cup.

Polynesian Pick-Up

Close your eyes and pretend you can hear the waves!

1 cup	papaya juice	250 mL
1 cup	Olympic Natural Yogurt	250 mL
2 tbsp.	coconut, grated	30 mL

Whirl until smooth. Makes 2 cups.

Yogurt Julep

Refreshing!

1 cup	Olympic Natural Yogurt	250 mL
1/2 cup	cold water	125 mL
	salt	
1 tsp.	fresh mint	5 mL
	mint leaves for garnish	

Blend until smooth and garnish with mint leaves. Pour over ice. Serves 2.

Yogurt Sip

After one sip, you'll be taking mouthfuls!

10 oz. pkg.	frozen peach slices	300 mL
1 cup	Olympic Natural Yogurt	250 mL
1/4 cup	Peach Brandy	60 mL
1/4 cup	light rum	60 mL
1 tbsp.	honey	15 mL
	ground nutmeg	

Thaw peaches at room temperature for 10 minutes. Meanwhile combine yogurt, brandy, rum and honey. Add peaches and syrup and blend until smooth. Pour into glasses and sprinkle with nutmeg. Makes five 4 oz. servings.

Strawberry Fizz

Use Ginger Ale if you prefer!

1 cup	strawberries, sliced	250 mL
1 cup	Club Soda	250 mL
1 cup	Olympic Natural Yogurt	250 mL
2 tbsp.	honey	30 mL

Mix in blender until smooth. Makes 3 cups.

Orange Smoothie

Better double this as they'll all want seconds!

6 oz.	tin frozen orange juice concentrate	185 mL
1 cup	Olympic Natural Yogurt	250 mL
1 cup	water	250 mL
1/4 cup	sugar	60 mL
1/2 tsp.	vanilla	2 mL
10	ice cubes	10

Place ingredients in a blender and whirl until smooth. Yield is 6 servings.

CAKES, COOKIES & DESSERTS

Raspberry Dessert

Even those who don't eat dessert can't resist this one!

Crust

2 cups	graham wafer crumbs	500 mL
1/2 cup	sugar	125 mL
1/4 cup	butter, melted	60 mL

Mix together and press into a greased pie pan.

Filling

1 cup	Olympic Natural Yogurt	250 mL
1/3 cup	sour cream	75 mL
1 tsp.	vanilla	5 mL
2	eggs, beaten	2
1 cup	sugar	250 mL
1/3 cup	flour	75 mL
3 cups	raspberries, fresh or frozen (drain if frozen)	750 mL

Whisk in yogurt, sour cream and vanilla to eggs. Mix sugar and flour and add to egg mixture. Gently stir in raspberries and pour into prepared pie shell. Bake at 400° F. (200°C) for 30 to 35 minutes or until center is almost set.

Topping

1/2 cup	brown sugar, packed	125 mL
1/2 cup	flour	125 mL
1/2 cup	walnuts	125 mL
1/4 cup	butter	60 mL

Mix brown sugar, flour, walnuts together and cut in butter until mixture is crumbly. Sprinkle over pie and return to oven for 10 minutes. Serve hot or cold. Makes a large dessert.

Strawberry Supreme

An elegant dinner party dessert!

1 cup	raspberries	250 mL
1 tbsp.	cold water	15 mL
2 cups	strawberries, sliced	500 mL
2/3 cup	whipping cream	150 mL
2/3 cup	Olympic Natural Yogurt	150 mL
4	meringue shells, finely crushed	4
6	strawberries, for garnish	6

Toss raspberries with the water in a pan over low heat until the juices draw and the fruit begins to fall. Cool, then press the puree through a fine sieve. Arrange the sliced strawberries in the bottom of a glass bowl and spoon the puree over. Mix the cream and yogurt together and whip until the mixture reaches the soft peak stage. Spread over the strawberries and level the top. Sprinkle a layer of the crushed meringue over the cream and garnish with the strawberries.
Serves 6.

Note: To elaborate, make four or five incisions in each strawberry and fan the pieces out by pressing gently with your finger.

Blueberry Challenge

We challenge you to resist seconds!

1/3 cup	butter, melted	75 mL
1/2 cup	sugar	125 mL
2	eggs	2
1 tsp.	rum or rum extract	5 mL
2 cups	flour	500 mL
1 tsp.	baking powder	5 mL
1/2 tsp.	baking soda	2 mL
1/2 tsp.	salt	2 mL
1/2 cup	Olympic Natural Yogurt	125 mL
1/4 cup	semi-sweet chocolate, shaved	60 mL
1-1/2 cups	blueberries, fresh or frozen	375 mL
1/2 cup	icing sugar	125 mL

Mix butter, sugar, eggs and rum. Add flour, baking powder, baking soda and salt and mix well with a wooden spoon. Stir in yogurt. Butter a 9" pie pan and place half the mixture on the bottom. Sprinkle with 2 tbsp. shaved chocolate, blueberries and icing sugar. Cover with remaining mixture. Sprinkle with remaining shaved chocolate. Bake at 350° F. (180°C) for 1-1/4 hours.

Spiced Apples

You had better double the recipe. They'll all want more!

1 lb.	cooking apples	500 g
6 tbsp.	butter	90 mL
1/4 cup	brown sugar, packed	60 mL
1 tsp.	cinnamon	5 mL
1/4 cup	port or sherry	60 mL
1/4 cup	Olympic Natural Yogurt	60 mL
1/4 cup	raisins	60 mL

Core and slice apples thickly. Cook slices in hot butter, stirring continuously until soft and golden brown. Add sugar, cinnamon and port and cook another five minutes. Remove from heat and fold in yogurt and raisins. Spoon into sherbet glasses and serve hot or chilled. Serves 4.

Banana Orange Fluff

Cool and refreshing!

1 tbsp.	unflavored gelatin (1 envelope)	15 mL
1/2 cup	orange juice	125 mL
1 tsp.	grated orange zest	5 mL
1 cup	Olympic Natural Yogurt	250 mL
1/2 cup	banana, pureed	125 mL
1/2 cup	sugar	125 mL
1/2 cup	evaporated milk	125 mL
2 tbsp.	orange juice	30 mL

Sprinkle gelatin over 1/2 cup (125 mL) orange juice in saucepan. Let stand 5 minutes to soften. Stir in orange zest and cook over low heat until gelatin is dissolved. Remove from heat. Stir in yogurt, banana puree and sugar. Chill to consistency of unbeaten egg white. Meanwhile, pour evaporated milk into an 8" metal cake pan. Chill in freezer until soft ice crystals form around edges of pan, about 10 or 15 minutes. Pour into a chilled small mixer bowl. Add 2 tbsp. (30 mL) orange juice and beat at high speed until stiff peaks form, about 2 minutes. Fold into banana mixture and chill until set. Makes 6 cups.

Grapes with Gingered Yogurt

An excellent light dessert!

1 cup	Olympic Natural Yogurt	250 mL
	chopped preserved ginger and syrup	
1/2 cup	seedless green grapes	125 mL

Combine and serve chilled. Serves 2.

Apple Ginger Cobbler

An easy microwave dessert!

Bottom layer

4	apples, peeled and sliced	4
1/2 cup	brown sugar, lightly packed	125 mL
1 tsp.	cornstarch	5 mL
2 tbsp.	water	30 mL
1 tbsp.	lemon juice	15 mL
1/2 tsp.	cinnamon	2 mL

Combine ingredients for apple layer in 8" round glass cake dish. Microwave on full power, covered 4 to 5 minutes or until apples are tender crisp, stirring once during cooking.

Top layer

1	egg	1
1/2 cup	Olympic Natural Yogurt	125 mL
1/4 cup	molasses	60 mL
2 tbsp.	oil	30 mL
1 cup	flour	250 mL
1/4 cup	brown sugar	60 mL
1/2 tsp.	baking soda	2 mL
1/2 tsp.	ginger	2 mL
1/4 tsp.	salt	1 mL
1/4 tsp.	baking powder	1 mL
1/4 tsp.	nutmeg	1 mL
	whipping cream (optional)	

Beat together egg, yogurt, molasses and oil. Add remaining ingredients and beat until smooth. Pour over apples. Microwave on full power, uncovered 6 or 7 minutes or until a toothpick inserted near the center comes out clean. Rotate dish during cooking. Serve warm or cold, with or without whipping cream. Makes 6 servings.

Chocolate Orange Cheesecake

All the best things combined into one!

1/4 cup	butter, melted	60 mL
1 cup	graham wafer crumbs	250 mL
1 tbsp.	cocoa	15 mL
2 tbsp.	sugar	30 mL
1 pkg.	cream cheese, softened	250 g
1	egg, lightly beaten	1
1/3 cup	sugar	75 mL
1/3 cup	Olympic Natural Yogurt	75 mL
10 oz.	can mandarin orange slices	284 mL
2 oz.squares	semi sweet chocolate	56 g
1 tsp.	butter	5 mL

Combine butter, graham crumbs, cocoa and 1 tbsp. (15 mL) sugar in bowl and mix well. Press evenly over bottom and sides of pie plate to make crust. Bake at 350° F. (180°C) for 8 to 10 minutes. Cool. Combine cream cheese, egg, sugar and yogurt in mixing bowl and beat until smooth. Drain oranges well and select 12 attractive pieces and reserve for garnish. Fold remaining orange slices into cream cheese mixture and pour into cooled pie shell. Bake uncovered at 350° F. (180°C) for 35 to 40 minutes or until center is set. Cool. Arrange reserved orange slices in a decorative pattern on cheesecake. Melt Chocolate and butter together and drizzle over top. Chill until serving time.

Substitute Olympic Natural Yogurt for milk in instant pudding mixes!

Raisin Meringue Pie

The way to a man's heart is by baking this pie for him!

1	9" baked pie shell	1
1-1/2 tbsp.	cornstarch	22 mL
1 cup	sugar	250 mL
1/4 tsp.	salt	1 mL
1/2 tsp.	nutmeg	2 mL
1-1/2 cups	Olympic Natural Yogurt	375 mL
3	egg yolks	3
1-1/2 cups	raisins	375 mL
1 tbsp.	lemon juice	15 mL

Mix cornstarch, sugar, salt and nutmeg in medium saucepan. Blend in yogurt. Stir in egg yolks, raisins and lemon juice. Cook over medium heat stirring constantly until mixture thickens and boils. Boil and stir 1 minute. Pour into pie shell.

Meringue

3	egg whites	2
1/4 tsp.	cream of tarter	1 mL
6 tbsp.	brown sugar	90 mL
1/2 tsp.	vanilla	2 mL

Beat egg whites and cream of tarter until foamy. Beat in brown sugar, 1 tbsp. (15 mL) at a time. Continue beating until stiff and glossy. Beat in vanilla. Heap brown sugar meringue onto hot pie filling, spreading to edge of crust to seal. Bake until lightly browned, about 10 minutes at 400° F. (200°C). Cool.

Luscious Lemon Pie

Always popular!

1 cup	graham wafer crumbs	250 mL
3 tbsp.	sugar	45 mL
1/4 cup	butter, melted	60 mL
1 tbsp.	unflavored gelatin (1 envelope)	15 mL
1/2 cup	water	125 mL
1 cup	Olympic Natural Yogurt	250 mL
1/2 cup	sugar	125 mL
1 tsp.	grated lemon zest	5 mL
	yellow food coloring	
1/2 cup	evaporated milk	125 mL
2 tbsp.	lemon juice	30 mL

Combine wafer crumbs, 3 tbsp. (45 mL) sugar and melted butter. Press into bottom and sides of a 9" pie plate. Bake at 375° F. (190°C) for 8 minutes. Chill. Sprinkle gelatin over water in a small saucepan. Let stand 5 minutes to soften. Cook and stir over low heat until gelatin is dissolved. Remove from heat, cool slightly. Stir in yogurt, 1/2 cup (125 mL) sugar, lemon zest and a few drops of food coloring. Chill to consistency of unbeaten egg white. Meanwhile pour evaporated milk into a 8" metal cake pan. Chill in freezer until soft ice crystals form around edges of pan (10 to 15 minutes). Pour into a chilled small mixer bowl. Add lemon juice and beat on high until stiff peaks form (about 2 minutes). Fold into gelatin mixture. Spoon into crumb crust and chill until set.

Cherry Pie

Martha would have loved this version!

Crust

1/3 cup	butter	75 mL
1-1/3 cups	graham wafer crumbs	325 mL
1/4 cup	sugar	60 mL

Melt butter and mix in graham crumbs and sugar. Press into 9" pie plate and bake at 375° F. (190°C) for 8 minutes. Cool.

Filling

1 tbsp.	cherry flavored gelatin	15 mL
1 cup	boiling water	250 mL
1/2 cup	cherry juice (from cherries)	125 mL
14 oz.	tin cherries, pitted	398 g
1 cup	Olympic Natural Yogurt	250 mL

Dissolve gelatin in boiling water. Add reserved cherry juice. Chill until set to the consistency of egg whites. Stir in cherries and yogurt and pour into cooled crust. Chill until firmly set.

Key Lime Pie

Pour into a baked pie crust instead of the graham crust if you prefer!

2 cups	graham wafer crumbs	500 mL
1/2 cup	sugar	125 mL
1/4 cup	butter, melted	60 mL

1 tbsp.	unflavored gelatin (1 envelope)	15 mL
1/2 cup	skim milk	125 mL
3/4 cup	brown sugar	185 mL
3	eggs, lightly beaten	3
2 cups	Olympic Natural Yogurt	500 mL
1/3 cup	lime juice	75 mL
1 tbsp.	grated lime zest	15 mL
few drops	green food coloring	few drops

Mix the graham crumbs, sugar and butter together. Except for 1/4 cup, line a greased pie plate with the mixture pressing into the sides and the bottom. Bake at 350° F. (180°C) for 10 to 12 minutes. Cool. While the crust is baking, sprinkle the gelatin over the milk in a saucepan and let soften for 5 minutes. Add the sugar and heat, stirring until the sugar and gelatin are dissolved. Stir some of the hot mixture into the eggs, return to the saucepan and heat, stirring until the mixture thickens. Add the yogurt, lime juice, lime zest and food coloring and pour into the pie plate. Top with the remaining crumbs. Refrigerate overnight. Slice into 6 pieces.

Blueberry Flan

A cheesecake type dessert!

1-1/2 cups	flour	375 mL
1/2 cup	sugar	125 mL
1-1/2 tsp.	baking powder	7 mL
1/3 cup	soft butter	75 mL
2	egg whites	2
1 tsp.	vanilla	5 mL
3 cups	blueberries, fresh or frozen	750 mL
2 tbsp.	flour	30 mL
2 cups	Olympic Natural Yogurt	500 mL
2	egg yolks	2
2/3 cup	sugar	150 mL
2 tsp.	grated lemon zest	10 mL
1 tsp.	vanilla	5 mL

Combine flour, sugar, baking powder, butter, egg whites and vanilla and mix well. Press into bottom of square cake pan, springform or flan pan. Sprinkle blueberries over top. Mix flour, yogurt, egg yolks, sugar, zest and vanilla and mix until smooth. Pour over berries. Bake at 350° F. (180°C) for 70 minutes or until golden. Serve warm or cold. Serves 10 to 12.

Poppy Seed Cake

Good with or without topping!

3/4 cup	poppy seeds	185 mL
1 cup	Olympic Natural Yogurt	250 mL
3/4 cup	oil	185 mL
1-1/2 cups	brown sugar	375 mL
2 cups	flour	500 mL
2 tsp.	baking powder	10 mL
1/4 tsp.	baking soda	1 mL
pinch	salt	pinch
3	egg whites, beaten stiff	3

1 cup	whipping cream	250 mL
1/4 cup	sugar	60 mL
2 tsp.	vanilla	10 mL
3 tsp.	cocoa	15 mL

Soak poppy seeds in yogurt for several hours. Blend oil and brown sugar together and add to yogurt. Sift together flour, baking powder, baking soda and salt. Mix dry ingredients with yogurt mixture and fold in beaten egg whites. Pour batter into loaf pans and bake at 350° F. (180°C) for 30 minutes. For topping whip cream, add sugar, vanilla and cocoa and mix well. Ice cake just before serving. Makes two loaves.

Butter Tart Slices

This freezes well (if there is any left!)

1/2 cup	butter	125 mL
1/4 cup	brown sugar	60 mL
1-1/4 cups	flour	300 mL

1/3 cup	butter	75 mL
2 tbsp.	Olympic Natural Yogurt	30 mL
1 tsp.	vanilla	5 mL
1 cup	brown sugar	250 mL
1 tbsp.	flour	15 mL
1	egg, beaten	1
1 cup	raisins	250 mL
1 cup	pecans, chopped	250 mL

Cream butter and sugar together and add flour. Press into a pan. Bake at 350° F. (180°C) for 15 minutes. Mix together the butter, yogurt, vanilla, sugar and flour. Blend in the egg. Add the raisins and pecans and mix well. Spread over the base. Bake at 275° F. (140°C) for 25 minutes. Makes approximately 36 squares.

Cranberry Streusel Cake

And you thought cranberries only went with turkey!

3/4 cup	brown sugar, lightly packed	185 mL
1/2 cup	all purpose flour	125 ml
1 tsp.	cinnamon	5 mL
1/4 cup	butter	60 mL
1/2 cup	soft butter	125 mL
1 cup	sugar	250 mL
2	eggs	2
1 tsp.	vanilla	5 mL
2 cups	all purpose flour	500 mL
1 tsp.	baking powder	5 mL
1 tsp.	baking soda	5 mL
1 cup	Olympic Natural Yogurt	250 mL
2 cups	cranberries, fresh or frozen	500 mL

Mix together brown sugar, 1/2 cup (125 mL) flour and cinnamon. Blend in 1/4 cup (60 mL) butter until crumbly and set aside. Cream 1/2 cup (125 mL) butter with white sugar until light and fluffy. Beat in eggs, one at a time, then add vanilla. Sift together flour, baking powder and baking soda and add to creamed mixture alternately with yogurt. Spread half the batter in a greased and floured spring form pan. Sprinkle with half the streusel mixture, then half the cranberries. Spread with remaining batter. Sprinkle evenly with remaining berries, then remaining streusel. Bake in a 350° F. (180°C) oven for one hour or until toothpick comes out clean when inserted in center. Cool in pan for 10 minutes before removing.

Whip Olympic Natural Yogurt with egg whites for a quick dessert topping!

Spice Cake

Top with Penuche Frosting -- a combination made in Heaven!

2 cups	all purpose flour	500 mL
1-1/2 cups	brown sugar, packed	375 mL
1-1/4 tsp.	baking soda	6 mL
1 tsp.	baking powder	5 mL
1/2 tsp.	salt	2 mL
2 tsp.	cinnamon	10 mL
1 tsp.	cloves	5 mL
1/2 tsp.	nutmeg	2 mL
1/4 cup	butter, softened	60 mL
1/4 cup	shortening	60 mL
2	eggs	2
1 cup	Olympic Natural Yogurt	250 mL
1/2 cup	water	125 mL
1 cup	raisins, chopped	250 mL
1/2 cup	walnuts, chopped	125 mL

Grease and flour oblong pan or two round layer pans. Mix all ingredients into large mixing bowl and combine for 2 minutes on low speed. Beat 3 minutes on high, scraping bowl occasionally. Pour batter into pan(s) and bake at 350° F. (180°C) until toothpick inserted in center comes out clean, approximately 50 minutes. Cool.

Penuche Frosting

1/2 cup	butter	125 mL
1 cup	brown sugar, packed	250 mL
1/4 cup	milk	60 mL
2 cups	icing sugar	500 mL

Melt butter in saucepan and stir in brown sugar. Heat to boiling, stirring constantly over low heat for 2 minutes. Stir in milk and heat to boiling. Remove from heat and cool to lukewarm. Gradually stir in icing sugar. Place pan of frosting in bowl of ice water and beat until spreading consistency. If frosting becomes too stiff, heat slightly, stirring constantly. Spread over Spice Cake.

Chocolate Layer Cake

Use your favorite filling between layers and for the topping!

1/2 cup	milk	125 mL
3 squares	unsweetened chocolate	3 squares
1/2 cup	butter	125 mL
1-1/2 cups	sugar	375 mL
2	eggs	2
1 tsp.	vanilla	5 mL
1-3/4 cups	all purpose flour	425 mL
1/2 tsp.	salt	2 mL
1 tsp.	baking soda	5 mL
1 tsp.	baking powder	5 mL
1 cup	Olympic Natural Yogurt	250 mL

Heat milk and chocolate until melted. Cool slightly. In another bowl, cream butter and sugar and beat until fluffy. Add eggs and beat well. Stir in vanilla and chocolate mixture. Sift together flour, salt, baking soda and baking powder. Add dry ingredients alternately with yogurt to batter. Pour into two greased and floured layer cake pans and bake at 350° F. (180°C) for 30 to 35 minutes or until toothpick comes out clean. Cool cakes on wire racks.

Peachy Yogurt Squares

A peach of a deal!

1 tbsp.	peach flavored gelatin	15 mL
1 cup	boiling water	250 mL
1/2 cup	peach syrup (from peaches)	125 mL
1 can	sliced peaches	1 can
1 cup	Olympic Natural Yogurt	250 mL

Dissolve gelatin in boiling water and add peach syrup. Chill until the consistency of an egg white. Cut peaches into small pieces and add, along with yogurt, to gelatin mixture. Pour into 9" square pan. Chill until firmly set. Cut into squares to serve.

Cinnamon Coffee Squares

Using the alternatives suggested below, you can "tailor make" to suit your family's preferences!

2 cups	brown sugar	500 mL
2 cups	all purpose flour, sifted	500 mL
1/2 cup	butter	125 mL
1/2 tsp.	salt	2 mL
2 tbsp.	instant coffee	30 mL
1 tsp.	cinnamon	5 mL
1/4 tsp.	nutmeg	1 mL
1 tsp.	baking soda	5 mL
1 cup	Olympic Natural Yogurt	250 mL
1	egg	1
1/2 cup	chopped nuts (cashews, walnuts or almonds)	125 mL

Combine brown sugar, flour, butter, salt, coffee, cinnamon and nutmeg in a medium mixing bowl. Blend with pastry blender until mixture is crumbly and completely blended. Butter a 9" square cake pan generously, spoon in half the crumb mixture. Stir soda into yogurt and mix into remaining crumbs along with the egg. Pour batter over crumbs and sprinkle with chopped nuts. Bake in a 350° F. (180°C) oven for 40 to 45 minutes or until done. Serve warm topped with whipped cream or cool and serve with fruit or ice cream.

For an alternative, try omitting coffee and cinnamon and increase nutmeg to one teaspoon (5 mL). Or omit coffee, cinnamon and nutmeg and add 1/2 tsp. (2 mL) allspice and add 2 tsp. (10 ml) of grated orange zest to the yogurt and egg mixture.

Substitute Olympic Natural Yogurt for buttermilk in baking but thin with water.

Raisin Cookies

Always a hit!

	boiling water	
1 cup	raisins	250 mL
1/4 cup	shortening	60 mL
1/4 cup	butter	60 mL
1 cup	brown sugar, packed	250 mL
1	egg	1
1/2 tsp.	vanilla	2 mL
1/4 tsp.	nutmeg	1 mL
1/2 cup	Olympic Natural Yogurt	125 mL
2-1/4 cups	all purpose flour	560 mL
1 tsp.	baking soda	5 mL
1/2 tsp.	cream of tartar	2 mL
1/2 tsp.	salt	2 mL
	sugar	

Pour boiling water over raisins to plump them. Drain and let dry. Cream together shortening, butter and brown sugar. Beat in egg, vanilla and nutmeg. Stir in yogurt. Sift together flour, baking soda, cream of tartar and salt. Blend gently into creamed mixture. Stir in raisins. If mixture is too soft to roll, chill for about 20 minutes. Roll out dough on floured board to about 1/3" thickness. Cut out with 2" round cookie cutter. Place on lightly greased baking sheet and sprinkle with sugar. Bake in 350° F. (180°C) oven for 10 to 12 minutes or until light golden brown. Makes 2 dozen.

Apricot Nut Cookies

Experiment with other dried fruits!

1/2 cup	oil	125 mL
1 cup	brown sugar	250 mL
1 tsp.	vanilla	5 mL
2	eggs	2
3 cups	flour	750 mL
1-1/2 tsp.	baking powder	7 mL
1/2 tsp.	salt	2 mL
1 tbsp.	grated orange zest	15 mL
1 cup	Olympic Natural Yogurt	250 mL
1 cup	dried apricots, chopped	250 mL
1 cup	nuts, chopped	250 mL

Beat oil with brown sugar until light, add vanilla and eggs, one at a time, beating until light. Combine flour, baking powder, salt and orange zest. Mix well and add gradually to oil and brown sugar mixture, alternating with yogurt. Stir in apricots and nuts. Drop by teaspoonfuls onto greased baking sheet. Bake at 350° F. (180° C) for 12 to 15 minutes. Cool on racks. Yield: 4 dozen.

Chocolate Drop Cookies

Kids love them!

1-3/4 cups	all purpose flour, sifted	425 mL
1/4 tsp.	baking soda	1 mL
1/4 tsp.	salt	1 mL
1/2 cup	butter	125 mL
1 cup	sugar	250 mL
1 tsp.	vanilla	5 mL
1	egg	1
2 squares	unsweetened chocolate, melted	2 squares
1/3 cup	Olympic Natural Yogurt	75 mL
3/4 cup	walnuts, chopped	185 mL

Sift flour, baking soda and salt and set aside. Cream butter and gradually add sugar, beating until light and fluffy. Add vanilla and egg and beat well. Blend in chocolate. Alternately, add flour mixture and yogurt, mixing well after each addition. Fold in walnuts. Drop from spoon onto ungreased baking sheet. Bake at 350° F. (180°C) for 10 to 12 minutes. Makes 4 dozen.

Molasses Cookies

A nice spicy cookie!

1/2 cup	butter	125 mL
1/2 cup	sugar	125 mL
1/2 cup	Olympic Natural Yogurt	125 mL
2	eggs	2
1/2 cup	molasses	125 mL
3 cups	flour	750 mL
1/2 tsp.	cinnamon	2 mL
1/4 tsp.	cloves	1 mL
1 tsp.	baking soda	5 mL
1/2 tsp.	ginger	2 mL
1/4 tsp.	salt	1 mL
	sugar	

Cream butter and sugar together, add yogurt, eggs and molasses. Mix well. Sift together flour and remaining ingredients (except sugar), add to yogurt mixture and stir well. Form into rolls and place on wax paper. Put in refrigerator overnight or until thoroughly chilled. Slice and roll in sugar. Bake at 375° F. (190°C) for 10 to 12 minutes.

Cinnamon Cereal Chewies

Don't tell them they are good for them!

3/4 cup	brown sugar	185 mL
1/4 cup	butter	60 mL
1/2 cup	Olympic Natural Yogurt	125 mL
1/2 tsp.	vanilla	2 mL
1 cup	rolled oats	250 mL
3/4 cup	all purpose flour	185 mL
1/4 cup	wheat germ	60 mL
1/2 tsp.	baking soda	2 mL
1/2 tsp.	cinnamon	2 mL
1/4 tsp.	salt	1 mL
12	Maraschino cherries, halved	12

Cream sugar and butter together. Beat in yogurt and vanilla. Stir together oats, flour, wheat germ, baking soda, cinnamon and salt. Stir into creamed mixture. Drop by teaspoon onto greased cookie sheet. Press cherry half into top of each cookie. Bake at 375° F. (190°C) for 10 to 12 minutes. Cool on cookie sheet for one minute before removing to wire rack. Makes 2 dozen.

Yogurt Popsicles

A good-for-them snack!

1 cup	raspberries	250 mL
1 cup	Olympic Natural Yogurt	250 mL
1/3 cup	sugar	75 mL
1/2 tsp.	vanilla extract	2 mL

Puree raspberries in blender until almost smooth and set aside. In a medium bowl, stir yogurt until smooth, then add sugar and vanilla. Stir in berries until well blended. Pour into popsicle containers and freeze for several hours. Makes a dozen popsicles.

Soft Frozen Yogurt

See alternate suggestions for substituting your favorite flavors!

1 envelope	unflavored gelatin	1 envelope
1/2 cup	water	125 mL
1/2 cup	honey	125 mL
1/2 tsp.	vanilla	2 mL
2 cups	Olympic Natural Yogurt	500 mL

Sprinkle the gelatin over the water and let soften for 5 minutes. Add the honey and heat the mixture, stirring until the gelatin dissolves. Pour into a large bowl and cool. Add the vanilla, then beat the yogurt into the gelatin mixture until smooth. Pour into an ice cream pail and freeze, stirring several times to ensure even freezing. When frozen, break into chunks and beat with a mixer until smooth. Makes about 1 quart.

Note: If you have an ice cream maker, follow the manufacturer's instructions and pour into the ice cream maker instead of the pail.

Try adding grated fresh vegetables to Olympic Natural Yogurt and freezing in popsicle containers!

Fun Alternatives for Frozen Yogurt

Orange Yogurt

Dissolve the gelatin in 1/2 cup (125 mL) orange juice instead of the water. Cool by adding another cup (250 ml) orange juice and grated zest of one orange.

Pineapple Yogurt

In addition to the above, add an 8 oz. can crushed pineapple with juice and 1 tbsp. (15 mL) lemon juice along with the 1 cup (250 mL) orange juice.

Peachy Yogurt

Following the directions for Orange Yogurt, add 5 fresh large ripe peaches, pureed and 1 tbsp. (15 mL) lemon juice and only add an additional 1/2 cup (125 mL) orange juice.

Berry Yogurt

Add 1 cup (250 mL) fresh strawberries, raspberries, blueberries or any other berry (pureed) and add to the gelatin mixture along with the yogurt.

Avocado Yogurt

Add 4 small pureed avocados and 1 tsp. (5 mL) grated orange zest along with the yogurt.

Melon Yogurt

Try adding 1 cup (250 mL) cubed cantaloupe or honeydew melon along with 1 tbsp. (15 mL) orange juice. Puree fruit before adding.

Surprise Yogurt

Use your imagination and try any combination of fruits you have on hand.

Note: Try making popsicles with any of the above combinations.

FISH & SEAFOOD

Tangy Sole

Substitute Red Snapper just for the Halibut!

2 lb.	sole filets	1 kg
	lemon juice	
	lemon pepper	
	tarragon	
	paprika	
3	green onions, chopped	3
1	red pepper, chopped	1
1	green pepper, cut in long strips	1
1/4 lb.	mushrooms, sliced	125 g
1/2 cup	Parmesan cheese, grated	125 mL
1 cup	Olympic Natural Yogurt	250 mL
1 tsp.	flour	5 mL
dash	Tabasco sauce	dash
1 tbsp.	pimento	15 mL
1 tbsp.	butter	15 mL
	parsley and lemon slices for garnish	

Arrange sole filets on a greased baking dish. Sprinkle with lemon juice, lemon pepper, tarragon and paprika. Layer with green onions, red and green pepper and mushrooms. Combine Parmesan, yogurt, flour, Tabasco and pimento. Pour over fish and vegetable mixture and dot with butter. Bake in a 400° F. (200°C) oven for about 15 minutes or until fish becomes translucent and flakes easily with a fork. Garnish with parsley and lemon slices. Serves 4 to 6.

Tangy Sole, page 78

Filet of Sole L'Indienne

A touch of the Far East!

1 lb.	fresh filets of sole	500 g
1/4 cup	oil	60 mL
1/2 tsp.	tumeric	2 mL
1/2 tsp.	ground ginger	2 mL
1/2 tsp.	cardamon seed	2 mL
1/2 tsp.	anise seed	2 mL
1/2 tsp.	cumin seed	2 mL
2 tbsp.	onion, finely chopped	30 mL
1/2 cup	dry white wine	125 mL
1/4 cup	sour cream	60 mL
1 tsp.	salt	5 mL
1/4 tsp.	zest of lemon	1 mL
1 tbsp.	lemon juice	15 mL
1/4 cup	Olympic Natural Yogurt	60 mL
1 tsp.	flour	5 mL

Arrange filets in baking dish. Combine half the oil with the tumeric and ginger. Pour over fish, turning fish several times to coat completely. Let stand at room temperature for an hour. Crush the cardamon, anise and cumin seeds and blend thoroughly. Cook onions in remaining oil until golden. Add crushed seeds, wine, sour cream, salt, lemon zest and juice. Combine yogurt and flour and add to sour cream mixture. Spoon over fish. Bake in 350° F. (180°C) oven about 30 minutes or until fish is done. Spoon sauce over fish two or three times while fish is baking. Serves 4.

Mix Olympic Natural Yogurt with seafood dip and pour over shrimps!

Stuffed Filets of Cod

Easy and elegant!

12 oz.	cod or other white fish	350 g
	salt and pepper	
2	cloves garlic, minced	2
2 tbsp.	onion, finely chopped	30 mL
1/2 cup	English cucumber, finely chopped	125 mL
1/2 cup	fresh tomato, coarsely chopped	125 mL
2 tsp.	lemon juice	10 mL
1/4 cup	fine dry bread crumbs	60 mL
1 tsp.	dried dill	5 mL
1/2 cup	Olympic Natural Yogurt	125 mL
	fresh cucumber slices for garnish	

Dry filets and sprinkle with salt and pepper. Line a greased baking dish with half the filets. Combine garlic, onion, cucumber, tomato, lemon juice and bread crumbs. Arrange evenly over fish. Cover with remaining fish filets. Bake uncovered at 400° F. (200°C) for 25 minutes or until fish flakes easily with a fork. Spread yogurt dill sauce over fish, return to oven and bake an additional five minutes or until heated through. Garnish with fresh cucumber. Serves 2.

Mix Olympic Natural Yogurt with chili sauce and lemon juice and serve over crab!

Spinach Stuffed Sole

Low in calories but high in flavor!

2 cups	fresh spinach leaves, finely chopped	500 mL
1/2 cup	onion, finely chopped, divided	125 mL
1/4 cup	red pepper, finely chopped	50 mL
1	clove garlic, minced	1
3 tbsp.	dry bread crumbs	45 mL
2 tsp.	lemon juice	10 mL
1/4 cup	Olympic Natural Yogurt	60 mL
1/2 lb.	sole filets	250 g
2 tsp.	Parmesan cheese, grated	10 mL
1/4 tsp.	paprika	1 mL

Combine spinach, half the onion and half the red pepper in a microwave-safe dish. Sprinkle the vegetables with a little water. Cover and microwave on High for 4 minutes, stirring once until spinach is wilted and set aside. In same casserole dish, combine remaining onion, red pepper and garlic. Microwave on High for 1 minute until onion is limp. Add bread crumbs and lemon juice and stir. Spread yogurt over each filet then spoon bread crumb mixture onto center of each. Roll up and secure with a toothpick. Put filets in same container, cover and Microwave on High for 4 minutes. Place spinach mixture in the bottom of a serving dish and cover with rolled up fillets. Sprinkle with the Parmesan cheese and paprika. Cover and microwave on High for 30 seconds or until spinach mixture is heated through. Serve immediately. Serves 2.

Poached Salmon with Zucchini Mayonnaise

Colorful with a delicate flavor!

1/2 cup	dry white wine	125 mL
1/2 tsp.	tarragon	2 mL
1-1/2 cups	water	375 mL
1	large salmon fillet	1
1/2 cup	zucchini, chopped	125 mL
1/4 cup	mayonnaise	60 mL
1/4 cup	Olympic Natural Yogurt	60 mL
2 tbsp.	chives, chopped	30 mL

Combine wine, tarragon and 1-1/2 cups water and bring to a boil. Add fish. Return to boiling and reduce heat. Cover and simmer until fish flakes with a fork (approximately 8 minutes). Remove fish and arrange on serving plate. To prepare sauce, stir together zucchini, mayonnaise, yogurt and chives. Spoon over fish and serve! Serves 4.

Salmon Cakes

Excellent served with Avocado Salsa shown below!

7-1/2 oz.	tin salmon	213 g
1 tbsp.	mayonnaise	15 mL
1 tbsp.	Olympic Natural Yogurt	15 mL
1 tbsp.	lime or lemon juice	15 mL
1-1/2 cups	bread crumbs	375 mL
1 tsp.	Dijon mustard	5 mL
1/3 cup	chives, chopped	75 mL
1	egg, beaten	1
pinch	thyme	pinch
	salt and pepper	
2 tbsp.	butter or olive oil	30 mL

Flake salmon into mixing bowl along with juice and bones. Add mayonnaise, yogurt, lime juice, 1 cup (250 mL) bread crumbs, mustard and chives. Mix with fork until well blended. Add beaten egg, thyme, salt and pepper. Shape salmon mixture into four patties. Mixture will be very soft. Coat patties in remaining bread crumbs and cook in butter over medium heat about 5 minutes on each side or until nicely browned. Serves 4.

Avocado Salsa

Serve as an accompaniment to the Salmon Cakes (above)!

1	medium tomato, peeled and diced	1
3/4 cup	English cucumber, diced	200 mL
1/2	hot banana pepper, seeded and chopped	1/2
2 tsp.	onion, minced	10 mL
1	clove garlic, minced	1
2 tsp.	cilantro, chopped	10 mL
1/2	avocado, peeled and chopped	1/2
	juice of half a lime or lemon	
1/2 cup	Olympic Natural Yogurt	125 mL

Mix all ingredients together, taste for seasonings and adjust to taste. Cover and refrigerate until needed. Makes 1 cup (250 mL).

Salmon Stuffed Mini Pitas

Great instead of a sandwich!

7 oz. pkg.	mini pitas	200 g
7-1/2 oz.	tin salmon	213 g
1/4 cup	Olympic Natural Yogurt	60 mL
3 tbsp.	chopped fresh dill	45 mL
2	green onions, minced	2
	salt and pepper	
	leaf lettuce	

Cut pitas in half. In bowl combine salmon, including juice and bones, yogurt, dill, green onion, salt and pepper to taste and mix well. Line pita pockets with lettuce, spoon salmon mixture into each half and serve. Makes four halves.

Note: For a variation on the above, add shrimp, alfalfa sprouts and roll in lettuce leaf instead of spooning into pita bread.

Crab and Shrimp Meat Curry

Serve over Kokuho Rose rice for a nice texture!

	butter, melted	
1	onion, chopped	1
4	cloves garlic, finely minced	4
2 tsp.	tumeric	10 mL
1 tsp.	ground ginger	5 mL
1/4 cup	coriander	60 mL
2 tbsp.	cumin	30 mL
1/2 tsp.	mustard seed	2 mL
1 tsp.	red pepper flakes	5 mL
2 tbsp.	mint, chopped	30 mL
1 tsp.	cornstarch	5 mL
1-1/2 cups	Olympic Natural Yogurt	375 mL
1/4 cup	lemon juice	60 mL
1 lb.	shrimp meat	500 g
1 lb.	crab meat	500 g

Cook onion and garlic in butter until soft, add tumeric, ginger, coriander, cumin, mustard seed, red pepper flakes and mint. Cook 5 minutes. Add the cornstarch to the yogurt and mix well. Add to the onion mixture but do not boil. Remove from heat, stir in shrimp and crab meat and sprinkle with lemon juice. Serve over rice. Serves 4.

Salmon Nuggets with Piquant Sauce

Serve as a main course or as an appetizer!

7-1/2 oz.	tin salmon, mashed with juice	213 g
3	green onions, chopped	3
1 tbsp.	Olympic Natural Yogurt	15 mL
1 tsp.	lemon juice	5 mL
1-1/2 cups	fine bread crumbs	375 mL
1 tsp.	Dijon mustard	5 mL
1	egg, beaten	1
pinch	thyme	pinch
	freshly ground pepper	
1 tbsp.	butter	15 mL

Mix salmon, onions, yogurt, lemon juice, 1 cup (250 mL) bread crumbs, mustard, egg, thyme and pepper until well blended. Shape in 1" (2.5 cm) balls, then flatten slightly. Roll in remaining bread crumbs. Melt butter and brown nuggets over high heat, about 1-1/2 minutes on each side or until lightly browned. Serve with Piquant Sauce. Makes about 15 nuggets.

Piquant Sauce

The slight dill pickle flavor adds a nice contrast to the salmon!

1/2 cup	Olympic Natural Yogurt	125 mL
2 tbsp.	sour cream	30 mL
2 tbsp.	dill pickle, finely chopped	30 mL
1 tbsp.	fresh parsley, minced	15 mL
1 tsp.	Dijon mustard	5 mL
1 tsp.	fresh tarragon	5 mL

Combine all ingredients and mix thoroughly.

Dilled Cod Bake

The cheeses add a nice crispy coating!

1 lb.	cod fillets	500 g
1/2 cup	Olympic Natural Yogurt	125 mL
1 tbsp.	prepared mustard	15 mL
1/2	onion, finely chopped	1/2
1 tbsp.	dill weed	15 mL
2 tbsp.	mayonnaise	30 mL
	salt and pepper	
2 tbsp.	Parmesan Cheese	30 mL
1/2 cup	Cheddar Cheese, grated	125 mL
dash	paprika	dash

Place cod fillets in greased casserole dish. Combine yogurt, mustard, onion, dill weed, mayonnaise, salt and pepper and spread over the fish. Bake for approximately 30 minutes at 450° F. (230°C) or until fish flakes easily. Sprinkle the cheeses and paprika over the fish and broil for 1 minute.
Serves 4.

Gourmet Sea Scallops

Serve with a salad for a luncheon dish!

1-1/2 lb.	scallops	750 g
1-1/2 cups	dry white wine	375 mL
	salt and pepper	
2 tbsp.	olive oil	30 mL
1 tbsp.	cornstarch	15 mL
1 cup	Olympic Natural Yogurt	250 mL
1/2 cup	milk	125 mL
1/2 cup	mushrooms, sliced	125 mL
2 tbsp.	Swiss cheese, grated	30 mL
2 tbsp.	bread crumbs	30 mL
1 tbsp.	butter	15 mL

Combine scallops, wine, salt and pepper. Cover and bring to a boil over low heat and simmer gently for 5 minutes. Remove scallops, saving liquid. In same saucepan, heat oil. Stir in cornstarch, then add cooking liquid and milk, a little at a time. Mix thoroughly, then add yogurt, scallops and mushrooms. Cook for 5 minutes, stirring occasionally. Remove from heat and add cheese. Pour into casserole dish, sprinkle with bread crumbs, dot with butter and broil until brown.
Serves 4 to 6.

MEAT DISHES

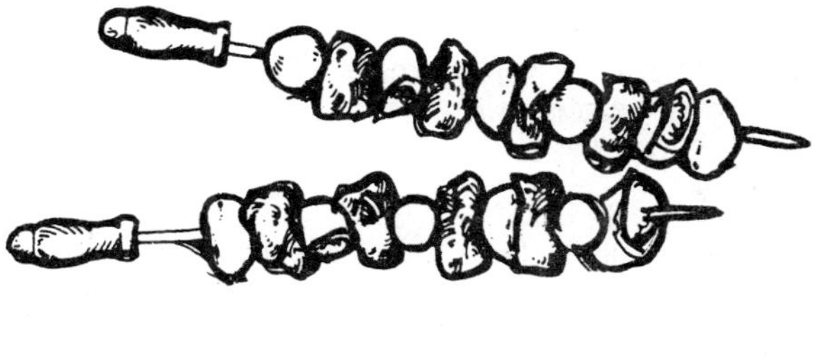

Meat Loaf

I have shared this recipe and friends agree it is the best meatloaf we have ever tasted!

1-1/2 lb.	ground beef	750 g
1/2 cup	dry bread crumbs	125 mL
1	egg	1
1 cup	Olympic Natural Yogurt	250 mL
1	small onion, chopped	1
1 tbsp.	Worcestershire Sauce	15 mL
1 tsp.	salt	5 mL
1/2 tsp.	dry mustard powder	2 mL
1/4 tsp.	pepper	1 mL
1/4 tsp.	sage	1 mL
1 clove	garlic, minced	1
1/2 cup	catsup	125 mL

Preheat oven to 350° F. (180°C). Mix all ingredients except catsup. Spread mixture in ungreased loaf pan approx. 9" x 5" x 3". Spoon catsup over loaf. Bake uncovered 1 to 1-1/4 hours. Let sit for 5 minutes and drain off fat before serving. Serves 6.

Pork and Cabbage Saute

Use your leftover pork roast! Your family will think you cooked for hours!

1/4 cup	oil	60 mL
2	onions, chopped	2
1	head cabbage, shredded	1
1/2 tsp.	salt	2 mL
1/4 tsp.	pepper	1 mL
1 tbsp.	paprika	15 mL
2 lb.	cooked pork, sliced	1 kg
1 cup	Olympic Natural Yogurt	250 mL
1 tsp.	cornstarch	5 mL

Heat half the oil, saute half the onions until golden brown. Add the cabbage and cook until tender. In another pan, heat remaining oil, saute rest of the onions. Add meat and continue cooking until brown. Cover and simmer over low heat about 10 minutes. Add cooked cabbage, stir well, then add salt, pepper, and paprika. Cook together for another 20 minutes. Remove from heat. Add cornstarch to yogurt and gradually stir into mixture. Serve immediately. Serves 4.

Gourmet Cutlets

The poppy seeds add the gourmet touch!

1 lb.	veal cutlets	500 g
1/2 tsp.	garlic salt	2 mL
1/4 tsp.	pepper	1 mL
1/4 cup	dry white wine	60 mL
1/4 cup	butter	60 mL
1	onion, chopped	1
	lemon slices	
1 tbsp.	poppy seeds	15 mL
2 cups	Olympic Natural Yogurt	500 mL
1 tsp.	cornstarch	5 mL

Cut meat into 1" cubes, season with garlic salt and pepper and marinate in wine four hours. Remove the veal and wipe carefully. Save the marinate. In a skillet, saute veal in butter 5 minutes. Add onion, lemon slices and poppy seeds and saute another 5 minutes, stirring continuously. Remove the veal and keep hot. Add the wine marinade, bring to a boil and reduce amount by 1/4. Add cornstarch to yogurt. Strain sauce and add to yogurt mixture. Pour into baking dish, add veal, cover and bake at 350° F. (180°C) for 45 minutes. Serves 4.

Nacho Bar-B-Que Bake

Try it today and mañana!

1 tbsp.	olive oil	15 mL
1 lb.	lean ground beef	500 g
1/4 cup	chopped onion	60 mL
4 oz.	can green chilies, drained and chopped	125 mL
1 cup	spicy Bar-B-Que sauce	250 ml
2	eggs	2
1-1/2 cups	Olympic Natural Yogurt	375 mL
2 cups	corn chips	500 ml
1/3 cup	red pepper, chopped	75 mL
1 cup	shredded Cheddar cheese	250 mL

Brown meat and onion in olive oil, drain. Stir in chilies and Bar-B-Que sauce. Mix well and spoon into 8 cup (2 L) baking dish. Combine eggs and yogurt and mix well. Spread over meat mixture. Top with corn chips and red pepper. Bake at 350° F. (180°C) for 25 minutes. Top with cheese and continue baking until cheese is melted. Let stand 5 minutes before serving. Serves 6.

Swedish Meatballs

A Swedish tradition on Christmas Eve!

1 lb.	ground veal	500 g
1 lb.	ground beef	500 g
1 lb.	ground pork	500 g
1	onion, chopped fine	1
3/4 cup	dry breadcrumbs	200 mL
1 tbsp.	minced parsley	15 mL
1/4 tsp.	nutmeg	1 mL
1/2 tsp.	allspice	2 mL
2 tsp.	salt	10 mL
1/4 tsp.	pepper	1 mL
1 tsp.	Worcestershire Sauce	5 mL
1	egg	1
1/2 cup	Olympic Natural Yogurt	125 mL
1/4 cup	olive oil	60 mL
1 tbsp.	butter	5 mL
1/4 cup	flour	60 mL
1 tsp.	paprika	5 mL
1/2 tsp.	salt	2 mL
1/8 tsp.	pepper	.5 mL
2 cups	water	500 mL
3/4 cup	Olympic Natural Yogurt	200 mL
1 tsp.	cornstarch	5 mL

Mix veal, beef, pork, onion, breadcrumbs, parsley, nutmeg, allspice, salt, pepper, Worcestershire Sauce, egg and yogurt together. Shape into small balls. Heat olive oil in skillet, add meatballs and brown well on all sides. Lift out meatballs as they brown. When all the meatballs are done, add butter to the drippings. Sprinkle in flour, paprika, salt and pepper. Let bubble, stirring occasionally. Add water and stir to blend. Bring to a boil, stirring constantly. Add meatballs and simmer 20 minutes. Mix cornstarch into yogurt and gradually add 1/2 cup hot mixture to yogurt stirring vigorously. Add yogurt mixture gradually to the hot gravy, simmer until hot and serve. Makes many meatballs.

Swedish Meatballs, page 92

Stew and Dumplings

Substitute lamb if you wish!

3 tbsp.	olive oil	45 mL
1-1/2 lb.	stewing beef, trimmed and cubed in 1/2" pieces (1.3 cm)	750 g
3 tbsp.	butter	45 mL
3	medium onions	3
3	cloves garlic	3
5	carrots	5
3	potatoes	3
2	stalks celery	2
2 cups	beef stock	500 mL
1 cup	white wine	250 mL
1 cup	tomatoes	250 mL
1 tsp.	salt	5 mL
1/4 tsp.	pepper	1 mL
1 tsp.	paprika	5 mL
1/4 tsp.	nutmeg	1 mL
1/4 cup	sour cream	60 mL
1/4 cup	Olympic Natural Yogurt	60 mL

Brown meat in oil. Melt butter and add onions and garlic. Cook until limp and add to meat. Add carrots, potatoes, celery and beef stock. Add wine, tomatoes, salt, pepper, paprika, and nutmeg and stir well. Reduce heat to low, cover and simmer for one hour, stirring occasionally. Remove from heat. Mix sour cream and yogurt together and gradually add hot liquid from stew until it is mixed well. Gradually add back to the stew. Serves 6.

Dumplings

The secret to good dumplings is to cover and don't peek!

1 cup	cake flour	250 ml
2 tsp.	double acting baking powder	10 mL
1/2 tsp.	salt	2 mL
1	egg	1
	milk	
1/3 cup	Olympic Natural Yogurt	75 mL
1/4 cup	finely chopped herbs	60 mL

Sift flour, baking powder and salt together. Break egg into measuring cup and add milk until the cup is half full. Beat well and stir the liquid slowly into the sifted ingredients. Add yogurt. Add more milk if necessary but keep the batter as stiff as possible. Add herbs. To drop batter from a spoon easily, dip the spoon into the hot stew first, then dip the spoon in the batter, fill it and drop the batter onto the stew. Continue until the dumplings are barely touching. Cover and simmer 30 minutes without removing lid. Serve at once.

Beer Stew

A refreshing change from Irish Stew!

2 tbsp.	olive oil	30 mL
1 lb.	boneless pot roast, cubed	500 g
2	onions, chopped	2
2	cloves garlic, minced	2
2 tbsp.	flour	30 mL
1 tsp.	honey	5 mL
1/2 cup	white wine	125 mL
1	cube Oxo	1
1 cup	beer	250 mL
1 cup	Olympic Natural Yogurt	250 mL
1	bay leaf	1
1/2 tsp.	pepper	2 mL
	salt	

Heat oil in large, heavy pan. Add meat and brown well on all sides. Remove and reserve. Add onions and garlic to pan and saute lightly. Stir in flour and honey, mix well and cook until browned. Blend together wine, Oxo, beer and yogurt and stir into onion mixture. Continue to stir until boiling. Add meat, bay leaf, pepper and salt. Cover tightly and simmer 2-1/2 to 3 hours or until meat is tender. Serves 6.

Ham and Potato Casserole

The Bridge Club will love it!

5	green onions, chopped	5
2	stalks celery, chopped	2
2	cloves garlic, minced	2
1 tbsp.	butter	15 mL
3	large potatoes, peeled and cubed	3
2 cups	cooked ham, chopped	500 mL
10 oz.	can Cream of Mushroom soup*	284 mL
1/4 cup	Olympic Natural Yogurt	60 mL
1 tsp.	thyme	5 mL
dash	ginger	dash
1 cup	grated Cheddar cheese	250 mL

Saute green onions, celery and garlic in butter until soft. Put the potatoes into a lightly greased 2 quart (2 L) casserole. Add ham, soup, yogurt, thyme and ginger and stir until well blended. Stir in onion mixture. Cover and bake for 1 hour at 350° F. (180°C). Sprinkle cheese on top and bake uncovered for 10 more minutes. Serves 4 to 6.

* Note: Any cream soup may be used.

Avocado Beef Dinner

The avocado adds a nice touch!

1-1/2 lb.	ground beef	750 g
1 tbsp.	olive oil	15 mL
1	onion, chopped	1
1/2 tsp.	salt	2 mL
1	clove garlic	1
1 tsp.	pepper	5 mL
10 oz.	can Cream of Mushroom soup	284 mL
1 cup	Olympic Natural Yogurt	250 mL
1	avocado, cubed	1
1/2	avocado, sliced	1/2
	lemon juice	
3 cups	cooked rice	750 mL

In a large skillet, lightly brown beef in olive oil. Add onion, salt, garlic and pepper. Cover and cook over low heat about 30 minutes. Blend in soup and cook another 5 minutes. Fold in yogurt and cubed avocado. Reheat. Garnish with avocado slices dipped in lemon juice and serve with hot rice. Serves 4 to 6.

Hamburgers Au Poivre

Dress up peppery hamburgers with the Shallot-Yogurt Sauce!

1 lb.	lean ground beef	500 g
2 tsp.	peppercorns	10 mL
1 tbsp.	oil	15 mL
1	shallot or green onion, finely chopped	1
1 tbsp.	red wine vinegar	15 mL
1/4 cup	Olympic Natural Yogurt	60 mL
1 tbsp.	parsley, finely minced	15 mL

Divide meat into 4 portions and shape into patties. Crush peppercorns using a rolling pin and spread out. Place patties on top pressing peppercorns into patties. Turn patties over and sprinkle any remaining peppercorns on top. Cook patties in oil, turning to brown both sides. Pour fat off, add shallots and wine vinegar and cook over medium heat, scraping up brown bits from bottom of pan. Remove from pan, add yogurt and stir to mix well. Stir in parsley. Spoon over patties. Makes 4 servings.

Pork Chops a l'Orange

Easy and excellent!

4	pork chops	4
	salt and pepper	
	paprika	
2 tbsp.	olive oil	30 mL
6 tbsp.	sugar	90 mL
2-1/2 tsp.	cornstarch	12 mL
1/4 tsp.	salt	1 mL
1/4 tsp.	cinnamon	1 mL
10	whole cloves	10
2 tsp.	grated orange zest	10 mL
1 cup	orange juice	250 mL
1/2 cup	Olympic Natural Yogurt	125 ml
1	orange, sliced	1

Sprinkle pork chops with salt, pepper and paprika and brown well in olive oil. Mix sugar, cornstarch, salt, cinnamon, cloves, zest, orange juice and yogurt and bring to a boil. Stir and cook until creamy. Add orange slices and serve over pork chops. Serves 2 to 4.

Combine Olympic Natural Yogurt with garlic and Dijon mustard for a zippy steak sauce!

Corned Beef Hash

Good for breakfast, lunch or dinner!

1	onion, finely chopped	1
1	red pepper, diced	1
1	green pepper, diced	1
6	green onions, chopped	6
1 stalk	celery, chopped	1 stalk
1 clove	garlic, minced	1 clove
1/2 lb.	mushrooms, sliced	250 g
6 tbsp.	butter	90 mL
1/2 cup	Olympic Natural Yogurt	125 mL
1	egg, beaten	1
1 lb.	corned beef, cooked and diced	500 g
3	potatoes, diced and cooked	3
1 tsp.	cumin	5 mL
1/3 cup	parsley	75 mL
1/2 tsp.	thyme	2 mL
1 tsp.	pepper	5 mL
	salt	
dash	Tabasco sauce	dash
1 tsp.	Worcestershire Sauce	5 mL

Saute onion, red and green pepper, green onion, celery, garlic and mushrooms in butter until vegetables are wilted. Blend together yogurt and egg and set aside. Mix rest of ingredients together and add to sauted vegetables. Add yogurt and egg mixture and mix well. Shape into patties and brown until cooked or turn the mixture into a frying pan and stir frequently until hot. Serves 4.

Use Olympic Natural Yogurt as a marinade for meat dishes!

Balkan Lamb & Eggplant Casserole (Moussaka)

You can use lamb or beef!

3 cloves	garlic, minced	3 cloves
2	onions, chopped	2
1	green pepper, chopped	1
1 tbsp.	olive oil	15 mL
1-1/2 lb.	ground lamb or beef	750 g
1-1/2 tsp.	salt	7 mL
	freshly ground pepper	
2 tsp.	paprika	10 mL
1 tbsp.	marjoram	15 mL
1 tbsp.	parsley	15 mL
1 tsp.	nutmeg	5 mL
2	eggplant, sliced	2
2 tbsp.	olive oil	30 mL
1/2 lb.	Monteray Jack cheese	250 g
1-1/4 cup	chicken stock	300 mL
1 cup	Olympic Natural Yogurt	250 mL
2	egg yolks	2
1 tbsp.	cornstarch	15 mL

Cook garlic, onion and green pepper in hot oil until limp. Add ground lamb and season with salt, pepper, paprika, marjoram, parsley and nutmeg. Remove mixture and set aside. In the same frying pan, fry eggplant slices in olive oil until golden. Layer half the eggplant in a greased casserole, top with half the meat mixture then half the cheese. Repeat layers. Pour chicken stock over casserole, cover and bake for 45 minutes at 350° F. (180°C). Mix yogurt, egg yolks and cornstarch together and pour mixture over casserole. Cover and continue to bake for another 15 minutes. Uncover and brown top under broiler. Serves 6.

Swedish Koldolma (Cabbage Rolls)

The yogurt keeps them moist!

1 lb.	ground beef	500 g
1/2 lb.	ground pork	250 g
1/2 lb.	ground veal	250 g
1	onion, chopped finely	1
1 clove	garlic, minced	1 clove
1 cup	cooked rice	250 mL
1 tsp.	salt	5 mL
	pepper	
1 tsp.	sugar	5 mL
1/2 tsp.	allspice	2 mL
pinch	nutmeg	pinch
1	egg	1
1/2 tsp.	dry mustard	2 mL
1 cup	bread crumbs	250 mL
1-1/2 cups	Olympic Natural Yogurt	375 mL
2 heads	cabbage, frozen or softened in boiling water	2 heads
	melted butter	
1 tbsp.	cornstarch	15 mL
1/2 cup	Olympic Natural Yogurt	125 mL

Mix all ingredients together down to cabbage. Put about 1 tbsp. mixture on cabbage leaf, roll up and fasten with a toothpick. Brown in butter and cook until meat is tender. When ready to serve, mix cornstarch with yogurt and gradually stir into frying pan. Add water to make a gravy.

Along with 1 tbsp. of cornstarch, add Olympic Natural Yogurt to pan drippings to make gravy.

PASTA & RICE

Pasta Prima Vera

Use the vegetables you have on hand!

2 cups	mixed vegetables (snow peas, cauliflower, broccoli, mushrooms, etc.)	500 mL
1/4 cup	olive oil	60 mL
4	green onions	4
1	clove garlic, finely chopped	1
2 tbsp.	flour	30 mL
1/2 tsp.	salt	2 mL
1/4 tsp.	freshly ground pepper	1 mL
1/2 tsp.	oregano	2 mL
1 cup	skim milk	250 mL
1 cup	Olympic Natural Yogurt	250 mL
1 tsp.	cornstarch	5 mL
4 cups	fettuccine noodles, cooked al dente	1 L
	Parmesan cheese	

Microwave vegetables five minutes and drain. Saute the green onions and garlic in the oil until tender but not browned. Sprinkle with the flour and cook for two minutes. Stir in salt, pepper, oregano and milk and bring to a boil. Continue stirring until thickened. Add cornstarch to yogurt and mix well. Gradually add some of the hot mixture to the yogurt and blend. Add yogurt mixture back into the sauce stirring continuously. Heat but do not boil. Add the vegetables and check the seasonings. Serve over noodles and sprinkle with freshly grated Parmesan cheese. Serves 4.

When adding Olympic Natural Yogurt to hot dishes, add just before serving and heat gently so as not to destroy the "friendly" bacteria!

Macaroni and Cheese

The kids will love it!

2 cups	macaroni, cooked al dente	500 g
2 cups	Cheddar cheese, grated	500 mL
1/4 cup	butter or margarine	60 mL
	salt and pepper	
1 cup	Olympic Natural Yogurt	250 mL
1 tsp.	hot mustard powder	5 mL
1 tsp.	Worcestershire Sauce	5 mL
1 tsp.	cornstarch	5 mL

In casserole, place one third of the macaroni and layer with one third of the Cheddar cheese. Dot with butter and sprinkle with salt and pepper. Mix remaining ingredients with yogurt and add one third of this mixture on top of the cheese. Continue layering with one third of each mixture at a time until all ingredients are used. Baked covered at 350° F. (180°C) for 30 minutes.
Serves 4 to 6.

Microwave Macaroni Casserole

Colorful and quick!

2 tbsp.	olive oil	30 mL
1	large onion, chopped	1
1	clove garlic, crushed	1
1	green pepper, chopped	1
1 cup	mushrooms, chopped	250 mL
1 lb.	minced steak	500 g
1/2 cup	tomato paste	125 mL
1 cup	Olympic Natural Yogurt	250 mL
dash	Tabasco Sauce	dash
2 cups	macaroni, cooked al dente or rotini or shells	500 mL
1/4 cup	grated Parmesan cheese	60 mL

Combine olive oil, onion, garlic, green pepper and mushrooms and cook on high for 5 minutes or until onion is soft and limp. Add steak and cook five minutes more or until meat is browned, stirring occasionally. Stir in tomato paste and cook on High 2 minutes. Stir in yogurt, Tabasco and pasta, sprinkle with cheese and reheat on High about 4 minutes to heat through. Serves 4.

Linguini Portofino

A delicious combination of shrimp and chicken!

2 tbsp.	olive oil	30 mL
4	shallots or green onions	4
1 cup	mushrooms, sliced (8)	250 mL
1/2 lb.	fresh shrimp	250 g
1/2 lb.	boneless chicken, cut in strips	250 g
1 cup	snow peas	250 mL
1 cup	dry white wine	250 mL
1/2 cup	Olympic Natural Yogurt	125 mL
1 tbsp.	cornstarch	15 mL
1/2 tsp.	salt	2 mL
1/2 tsp.	thyme	2 mL
1/8 tsp.	pepper	.5 mL
1	tomato, peeled and chopped	1
2 cups	linguini, cooked al dente	500 mL
	grated Parmesan cheese	

In a large skillet, cook shallots and mushrooms in olive oil for 5 minutes over medium heat. Add shrimp, cook until pink. Remove mixture from skillet and set aside. Cook chicken in remaining oil for 5 minutes. Add snow peas and cook 3 minutes. Return shrimp mixture to skillet. Stir in wine, deglazing the pan. Add the cornstarch to the yogurt and mix well. Gradually add some of the hot wine to the yogurt, then add back to the wine mixture along with the salt, thyme, pepper and tomato. Simmer about 5 minutes until slightly thickened. Spoon mixture over cooked pasta and top with Parmesan cheese. Serves 4.

Yoghetti

Quick and easy!

1/2 lb.	spaghetti, cooked al dente	250 g
1 tbsp.	butter	15 mL
1/4 cup	olive oil	60 mL
1	clove garlic	1
5-1/2 oz.	tomato paste	156 mL
	salt	
	pepper	
2 cups	Olympic Natural Yogurt	500 mL

Drain spaghetti and return to sauce pan. Add butter and toss lightly until spaghetti is well coated. In another pan, heat oil and saute garlic for 1 minute, add tomato paste, salt and pepper. Remove from heat, add yogurt and blend thoroughly. Pour sauce over the hot spaghetti. Serves 6.

Linguini Portofino, page 106

Beef Stroganoff

Always a favorite and this one is low in calories!

1 lb.	beef tenderloin	500 g
	pepper, freshly ground	
1/2 lb.	mushrooms, sliced	250 g
1	onion, sliced	1
1/4 cup	olive oil	60 mL
3 tbsp.	flour	45 mL
2 cups	beef broth	500 mL
1/4 cup	red wine or sherry	60 mL
1/2 tsp.	paprika	2 mL
dash	cayenne	dash
1 tsp.	dry mustard	5 mL
1 tsp.	oregano	5 mL
1 tsp.	dill weed	5 mL
1 tsp.	cornstarch	5 mL
	salt	
	pepper	
1 cup	Olympic Natural Yogurt	250 mL
3 cups	fettuccine noodles, cooked al dente	750 mL

Trim fat off meat and cut into thin strips, about 2" long. Sprinkle with pepper and let stand in a cool place for two hours. In a heavy skillet, saute mushrooms in oil until tender, remove and saute onions in the same oil until brown. Remove from skillet. Brown meat quickly on all sides until rare. Remove and set aside.
Blend the flour into the oil in the skillet and gradually add the broth, stirring constantly until smooth and slightly thickened. Combine the sauce with the meat, mushrooms, onions and red wine in the top of a double boiler and cook for twenty minutes. Add paprika, cayenne, dry mustard, oregano, dill weed, cornstarch, salt and pepper to the yogurt and mix well. Blend into the double boiler five minutes before serving and serve over wide noodles or your favorite pasta or rice. Serves 6.

Use Olympic Natural Yogurt often if you are on a low cholesterol way-of-life!

Rotelle with Ricotta and Mushrooms

Colored rotelle makes it even more appealing!

1 cup	Ricotta cheese	250 mL
1 cup	Olympic Natural Yogurt	250 mL
2 tsp.	cornstarch	10 mL
3/4 cup	rotelle (corkscrew) pasta, cooked al dente	185 mL
1 tbsp.	butter	15 mL
1	onion, chopped	1
1 clove	garlic, minced	1 clove
1 lb.	mushrooms, sliced	500 g
1 cup	tomatoes, chopped	250 mL
1 tsp.	salt	5 mL
1/4 tsp.	black pepper	1 mL
1/4 tsp.	sugar	1 mL

Process Ricotta cheese, yogurt and cornstarch in food processor until smooth. Melt butter in frying pan, add onion and garlic, cooking until onion is crisp, about 5 minutes. Add mushrooms, tomatoes, salt, pepper and sugar, stirring occasionally until mushrooms and tomatoes form a sauce, about 5 minutes. Stir in reserved ricotta mixture, cook and stir over low heat until mixture thickens slightly, about 4 minutes. Toss with pasta. Makes 4 servings.

Saute garlic in butter and mix with Olympic Natural Yogurt for a tasty pasta sauce!

Lasagna

A lighter, cheesy lasagna to entice all your senses!

12 - 14	lasagna noodles, cooked al dente	12 - 14
1 tsp.	olive oil	5 mL
1 lb.	lean ground beef	500 g
1	onion	1
1 cup	tomatoes (1 pint)	250 mL
dash	Tabasco	dash
1 tsp.	Worcestershire sauce	5 mL
14 oz.	tomato sauce	398 mL
5-1/2 oz.	tomato paste	156 mL
1 cup	mushroom pieces, drained	250
2	cloves garlic, minced	2
1 tsp.	each basil, oregano, rosemary and tarragon	5 mL
1 tsp.	salt	5 mL
1/4 tsp.	pepper	1 mL
1-1/2 cups	Olympic Natural Yogurt	375 mL
2 cups	cottage cheese	500 mL
10 oz.pkg.	frozen spinach, chopped and drained	300 g
1	egg	1
2 cups	shredded Mozzarella cheese	500 mL

Brown beef and onions in skillet, pour off excess fat. Add tomatoes, Tabasco, Worcestershire sauce, tomato sauce, tomato paste and mushrooms. Stir in garlic, basil, oregano, rosemary, tarragon, salt, pepper and yogurt. Heat through but do not boil. Combine cottage cheese, spinach and egg. In a 13" x 9" (33 cm x 23 cm) baking dish, alternate layers starting with beef mixture, then noodles, then cottage cheese and Mozzarella. Repeat layers ending with a cheese layer. Bake in 350° F. (180°C) oven for 30 minutes. Remove from oven and let stand 5 minutes before serving. Serves 10.

Cheesy Noodles Romanoff

Nutritious and simple to make!

1	medium onion, chopped	1
2	cloves garlic, minced	2
1 cup	mushrooms, sliced	250 mL
2 tbsp.	butter	30 mL
8 oz.	wide egg noodles, cooked al dente	250 g
1 cup	cottage cheese	250 mL
1 cup	Olympic Natural Yogurt	250 mL
1 tsp.	Worcestershire Sauce	5 mL
dash	Tabasco Sauce	dash
1 cup	Cheddar cheese, shredded	250 ml
1 cup	shrimp, tuna, salmon or ham	250 mL
	salt and pepper	
	bread crumbs	
	Parmesan cheese, grated	

Saute onions, garlic and mushrooms in the butter. In a 3 quart (3 L) casserole, combine mushroom mixture, noodles, cottage cheese, yogurt, Worcestershire Sauce, Tabasco Sauce, Cheddar cheese, fish or ham, salt and pepper. Top with bread crumbs and Parmesan cheese. Bake at 350° F. (180°C) for 25 minutes or until browned. Serves 6.

Wild Rice and Mushrooms

A nice change from plain rice!

3 tbsp.	olive oil	45 mL
1	onion, sliced	1
1/2 cup	mushrooms, sliced	125 mL
1 tsp.	salt	5 mL
1 tbsp.	minced parsley	15 mL
1-1/2 cups	wild rice	375 mL
2 cups	stock	500 mL
1 cup	sweet cider	250 mL
3/4 cup	Olympic Natural Yogurt	200 mL

Saute onion and mushrooms in olive oil. Add salt, parsley and rice. Stir until rice is coated with oil. Add 1 cup hot stock. Cover tightly and cook over low heat until liquid has been absorbed. Add remaining stock. When stock has been absorbed, add cider, and continue cooking, covered, until cider has been absorbed and rice is done. Remove from heat and blend in yogurt. Serves 6.

Persian Rice

This traditional dish is generally served cool!

1 tbsp.	oil	15 mL
2 tsp.	black mustard seeds	10 mL
2 tsp.	fresh ginger, finely minced	10 mL
4 cups	cooked rice, cooled	1 L
1-1/2 cups	Olympic Natural Yogurt	375 mL
2 tbsp.	green pepper, chopped	30 mL
1/8 tsp.	cayenne	.5 mL
1	bay leaf, crumbled	1

Add the mustard seeds to hot oil in a heavy skillet and cover. When the popping noise dies down (just a few seconds), add the ginger, rice, yogurt, green pepper, cayenne and bay leaf. Stir and cook gently for 5 minutes. Cool to desired temperature. Serves 4 to 6.

Saffron Rice

Saffron adds a touch of class!

1/2 lb.	long grain rice	250 g
1	egg	1
1 cup	Olympic Natural Yogurt	250 mL
6 oz.	almonds, chopped	200 mL
1/4 tsp.	Spanish saffron	1 mL
	salt and pepper	

Rinse rice for 1 minute in boiling water, then drain. Drop the rice into rapidly boiling salted water and cook for 10 minutes. Rinse in cold water and drain. Beat egg and mix with yogurt and half the cooked rice. Grease a casserole and put in yogurt rice mixture. Sprinkle with chopped almonds, then add a layer of rice. Repeat layers until all ingredients are used. Sprinkle with saffron, salt and black pepper. Bake at 375° F. (190°C) for 40 to 50 minutes. This will form a crust on the bottom of the casserole. Turn upside down and serve with the golden crust on top. Serves 4.

POULTRY

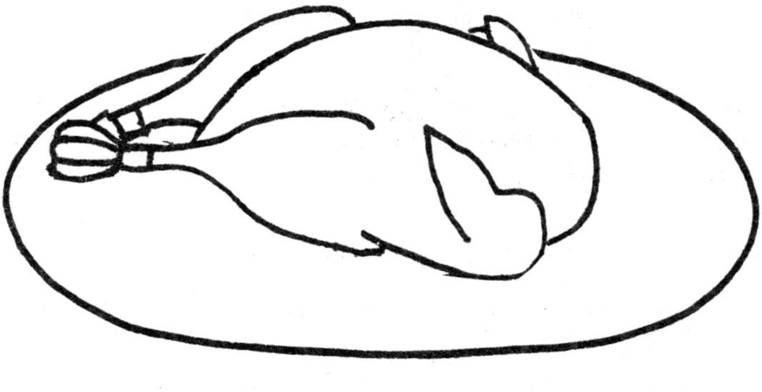

Curried Papaya Chicken

You'll want to eat this every night!

1-1/2 lb.	chicken parts, skinned	750 g
2-1/2 tsp.	flour, divided	7 mL
1 tsp.	curry powder, divided	5 mL
1/4 tsp.	salt	1 mL
1/4 tsp.	pepper	1 mL
2 tsp.	butter or olive oil, divided	5 mL
1/4 cup	onion, diced	60 mL
2 cups	chicken broth	500 mL
2 tbsp.	Olympic Natural Yogurt	30 mL
1/2	medium papaya, pared, seeded and cut into strips	1/2

Dry chicken. In a plastic bag combine 1-1/2 tsp. (7 mL) flour, 1/4 tsp. (2 mL) curry powder, salt and pepper and shake chicken in mixture until coated. Heat half the butter until bubbly, brown chicken. Remove the chicken. In same skillet, heat remaining butter, add onion and saute until softened, 1 to 2 minutes. Return chicken to skillet, add broth and bring to a boil. Reduce heat, cover and let simmer until chicken is tender, about 40 minutes. Add more water if necessary. Remove chicken to platter reserving juices. In a small bowl combine yogurt and remaining flour and curry powder, mixing well. Add to pan juices along with papaya. Cook, stirring gently until papaya is heated and sauce is thickened. Serve over chicken. Serves 2.

Chicken Dijon

The coating keeps it crisp and juicy!

6	chicken breasts, skinned	6
	salt and pepper	
1/4 cup	Dijon mustard	60 mL
1/3 cup	Olympic Natural Yogurt	75 mL
1/2 cup	fine bread crumbs	125 mL
1/2 tsp.	thyme	2 mL

Sprinkle chicken lightly with salt and pepper. Mix mustard with yogurt. In another bowl, mix bread crumbs, thyme, 1/2 tsp. (2 mL) salt and 1/4 tsp. (1 mL) pepper. Spread each piece of chicken with mustard mixture, then roll in bread crumb mixture. Place chicken on lightly greased baking sheet and bake in 350° F. (180°C) oven for 50 minutes (bone-in) or 35 minutes (boneless) or until golden brown and meat is no longer pink. Makes 6 servings.

Stuffed Chicken with Mushroom Sauce

A lot easier than stuffing the turkey and just as good!

4	chicken breasts, skinned and deboned	4
2 tbsp.	flour	30 mL
1 tsp.	salt	5 mL
dash	paprika	dash
1 cup	bread crumbs	250 mL
1	small onion, chopped	1
2 tsp.	poultry seasoning	10 mL
1/4 cup	hot water	60 mL
2 tbsp.	butter, melted	30 mL

Dust each breast with flour, salt and paprika. Combine bread crumbs, onion, poultry seasoning, and hot water. Spread mixture on breasts, roll up and fasten with toothpicks. Brown in butter in frying pan. Bake in oven at 325° F. (160°C) for one hour.

Sauce

1/2 lb.	fresh mushrooms, sliced	250 g
1/4 cup	onion, minced	60 mL
2 tbsp.	butter or olive oil	30 mL
2 tbsp.	flour	30 mL
	salt and pepper	
1-1/2 cups	Olympic Natural Yogurt	375 mL

Brown mushrooms and onions in butter. Stir in flour, salt and pepper. Add yogurt and cook very slowly until heated. Pour over chicken and serve!
Serves 4.

Use Olympic Natural Yogurt as a marinade for poultry!

Tarragon Chicken

A good microwave chicken recipe!

4	chicken thighs or drumsticks, skinned	4
2 tbsp.	flour	30 mL
2 tbsp.	oil	30 mL
1/2 cup	white wine (or grape juice)	125 mL
1/3 cup	chicken stock	75 mL
1 tsp.	fresh tarragon, chopped	5 mL
1/4 tsp.	ground marjoram	1 mL
2 cloves	garlic, crushed	2 cloves
1 cup	mushrooms, sliced	250 mL
1 tbsp.	cornstarch	15 mL
1/2 cup	Olympic Natural Yogurt	125 mL
1/4 cup	green onion, chopped	60 mL

Arrange chicken in a microwave-safe dish with thicker portions toward the outside of dish. Cover with lid or plastic wrap and cook 5 minutes on High. Combine flour and oil, stir in wine, chicken stock, seasonings and mushrooms. Cook 6 minutes on High until smooth and thickened, stirring once. Add cornstarch to yogurt and mix well. Add stock mixture gradually to yogurt stirring well. Add half the green onions. Pour the sauce over the drained chicken. Cover and cook 8 to 10 minutes on Medium power or until chicken is tender. Garnish with remaining onion. Let stand covered 5 minutes to finish cooking. Serves 2.

Barbecued Chicken Tika

Add an Oriental touch to your barbecued chicken!

6	chicken breasts	6
3 cups	Olympic Natural Yogurt	750 mL
2 tsp.	salt	10 mL
1-1/2 tsp.	ginger, ground	7 mL
2	cloves garlic, minced	2
1 tsp.	chili powder	5 mL
2 tbsp.	lemon juice	30 mL
1 tsp.	black pepper	5 mL
	red food coloring	
1/2 cup	oil	125 mL

Makes slits in chicken. Combine the rest of the ingredients and pour over the chicken. Cover and refrigerate overnight. Barbecue for approximately 30 minutes or until chicken is done. Makes 6 servings.

Tandoori Chicken

The marinating leaves this Indian dish moist and spicy with an appealing bright red color.

3 lbs.	chicken pieces, skinned	1.5 kg
4	garlic cloves, minced	4
1	onion, chopped	1
1/3 cup	lime juice	75 mL
1 tbsp.	paprika	15 mL
1/2 tsp.	freshly ground black pepper	2 mL
1 tsp.	cumin	5 mL
1 tsp.	coriander	5 mL
1/2 tsp.	cinnamon	2 mL
1 tsp.	cardamon	5 mL
1/4 tsp.	tumeric	1 mL
pinch	ground cloves	pinch
1	slice, peeled fresh ginger	1
1/4 tsp.	salt	1 mL
1-1/2 tsp.	Dijon mustard	7 mL
1 cup	Olympic Natural Yogurt	250 mL
1/4 cup	butter, melted for basting	60 mL
	lime wedges for garnish	

Make random cuts in the flesh of the chicken and place in an oven proof baking dish. Put remaining ingredients, except lime wedges and butter, in a blender and puree. Pour over the chicken. Cover the chicken and refrigerate for at least 6 hours or overnight, turning the pieces occasionally. Bake at 350° F. (180°C) for 45 to 60 minutes or until done, basting occasionally with melted butter. Garnish with lime wedges. Serves 6.

Note: Tandoori actually means "clay oven" but this dish turns out just fine baked in the regular oven!

If you would prefer a thicker base to some of your recipes, let Olympic Natural Yogurt sit in a strainer for several hours before measuring!

Chicken Sesame

Put in your slow cooker and forget about it until dinner!

1	frying chicken, cut up	1
1/4 cup	flour	60 mL
3 tbsp.	sesame seeds	45 mL
1/2 tsp.	salt	2 mL
1/4 tsp.	pepper	1 mL
1/4 cup	oil	60 mL
1	onion, chopped	1
2	stalks celery, chopped	2
1/2 cup	dry white wine	125 mL
1	cube, chicken bouillon	1
1/2 tsp.	tarragon	2 mL
1/4 cup	cornstarch	60 mL
1/4 cup	water	60 mL
1 cup	Olympic Natural Yogurt	250 mL

Coat chicken with mixture of flour, sesame seeds, salt and pepper. In large skillet, brown chicken in oil. Add onion, celery, wine, bouillon cube and tarragon. Cover and cook in slow cooker on low for 6 to 8 hours. Turn control to high, remove chicken to warm shallow dish. Dissolve cornstarch in water and stir into pot. Cook on high 15 minutes. Turn heat off and stir in yogurt. Pour sauce over chicken and serve with rice or noodles. Serves 5.

Honey and Curry Chicken

It smells as good as it tastes!

2/3 cup	butter, melted	150 mL
1 cup	liquid honey	250 mL
1/4 cup	prepared mustard	60 mL
2 tbsp.	curry powder	30 mL
1 cup	Olympic Natural Yogurt	250 mL
8	chicken breasts or legs	8

Mix butter, honey, mustard, curry powder and yogurt together. Roll chicken pieces in mixture coating well. Arrange in pan with bone side up. Cook at 375° F. (190°C) for 45 minutes turning chicken and basting with the sauce. Cook 15 minutes more or until chicken is tender. Serves 6 - 8.

Chicken Paprika

Just the right touch of "hot"!

2 tbsp.	olive oil	30 mL
4	chicken breasts, skinned	4
1	onion, sliced thinly and separated into rings	1
1	clove garlic, chopped	1
1 tsp.	paprika	5 mL
1 tbsp.	flour	15 mL
1 tsp.	salt	5 mL
1/2 tsp.	pepper, freshly ground	2 mL
1-1/2 cups	chicken broth	375 mL
1 cup	Olympic Natural Yogurt	250 mL
1 tbsp.	cornstarch	15 mL

Heat the oil and brown the chicken on both sides. Remove chicken to paper toweling and keep warm. Add the onions to the skillet and cook until golden. Add the garlic, paprika, flour, salt and pepper and cook, stirring for 2 minutes. Add the broth and bring to a boil. Return the chicken to the skillet, cover and simmer for 20 minutes or until cooked. Combine the yogurt and cornstarch and stir into the liquid in the skillet. Cook just until thickened but do not boil. Spoon the sauce over the chicken and serve. Serves 4.

To prevent Olympic Natural Yogurt from curdling in hot dishes, add 1 tbsp. cornstarch.

Chicken Souvlaki

Greek-style chicken in pita bread!

1 tbsp.	olive oil	15 mL
1 cup	Olympic Natural Yogurt	250 mL
1/2 cup	lemon juice	125 mL
1	clove garlic, minced and mashed to a paste with salt	1
pinch	salt	pinch
1/2 tsp.	dried thyme	2 mL
	lemon pepper	
8	boneless chicken thighs, skinned	8
	OR	
4	chicken breasts, cubed	4
1/3 cup	Olympic Natural Yogurt	75 mL
1 clove	garlic, minced and mashed to a paste with salt	1 clove
pinch	salt	pinch
	lemon pepper	
2 tsp.	lemon juice	10 mL
1 tbsp.	parsley, finely chopped	10 mL
2 tsp.	mint leaves, finely chopped	10 mL
1	red onion, sliced thin	1
2 tbsp.	olive oil	30 mL
1	tomato, minced	1
1 tbsp.	sesame seeds, toasted lightly	15 mL
6	whole wheat pita pocket bread	6

To make the marinade, whisk together the olive oil, yogurt, lemon juice, garlic, thyme and pepper. Arrange the chicken, pricked in several places with a fork, in a layer in shallow dish. Pour the marinade over it and let it marinate, covered at least 3 hours or overnight, turning once. To make the sauce, whisk together the yogurt, garlic paste, pepper, lemon juice, parsley and mint. Grill chicken on barbecue about 12 to 15 minutes on each side or until cooked through. While the chicken is cooking, cook onion in olive oil until it is lightly golden. Remove from heat and add tomato, sesame seeds, salt and pepper. When chicken is done, cut diagonally into thin slices. Heat pita bread on the grille for several seconds or until softened. Insert chicken, onion mixture and sauce into the pockets and serve. Serves 6.

Note: If using chicken breasts, thread cubes onto a wooden skewer and barbecue. (Soak the skewers in water for 20 minutes before threading).

Crispy Fried Chicken

Wait until the Colonel hears about this one! (The secret is the coating!)

3 lb.	frying chicken pieces	1.5 kg
1/4 tsp.	salt	1 mL
1/4 tsp.	pepper	1 mL
1 cup	Olympic Natural Yogurt	250 mL
1/2 cup	skim milk	125 mL
2 tsp.	honey	10 mL
1 tsp.	grated lemon zest	5 mL
1-1/2 cups	self-rising flour	375 mL
1 tsp.	paprika	5 mL
	oil for deep frying	

Sprinkle each chicken piece with salt and pepper. Combine the yogurt, milk, honey and lemon zest. In a pie plate, mix the flour and paprika. Dip each piece of chicken into the yogurt mixture and then into the flour. Deep fry until nicely browned on each side at a temperature of approximately 330° F. (166°C). Serves 4 - 6.

Chicken Breasts in Champagne

So easy you don't have to wait for a special occasion to try this!

2	chicken breasts, skinned	2
1/3 cup	flour	75 mL
1 tsp.	salt	5 mL
1/4 tsp.	pepper	1 mL
1/4 cup	butter	60 mL
2 tbsp.	olive oil	30 mL
1 cup	mushrooms, sliced	250 mL
1 cup	champagne	250 mL
1 tbsp.	cornstarch	15 mL
1 cup	Olympic Natural Yogurt	250 mL

Coat chicken breasts with mixture of flour, salt and pepper. Heat the butter and oil, saute the mushrooms and set aside. Add the chicken and saute for 5 minutes. Turn the chicken over and add the champagne. Cook for another 15 minutes or until the chicken is fully cooked and the champagne is reduced by half. Remove the chicken pieces to a heated serving platter and keep warm. Spoon the mushrooms over the chicken. Mix the cornstarch with the yogurt and gradually add to the juices in the frying pan. Heat until thickened, stirring continuously. Pour the sauce over the chicken and serve. Serves 2.

Basil Chicken

This is a favorite not only because it can be made ahead of time!

4	chicken breasts, skinned	4
3/4 cup	Olympic Natural Yogurt	185 mL
1/2 cup	fresh basil, chopped	125 mL
2 tsp.	cornstarch	10 mL
	salt and pepper	
1/4 cup	Parmesan cheese, grated	60 mL
1 cup	bread crumbs	250 mL

Arrange chicken in baking dish. Combine yogurt, basil and cornstarch, mix well and spread over chicken. Add salt, pepper and Parmesan cheese to bread crumbs and sprinkle over chicken. (Can be refrigerated for up to six hours). Bake at 375° F. (190°C) for 30 minutes or until chicken is no longer pink inside. Serves 4.

Cinnamon Chicken Bake

The cinnamon adds an intriguing taste!

2/3 cup	cornflake crumbs	150 mL
1 tbsp.	brown sugar	15 mL
2 tsp.	ground cinnamon	10 mL
2 tsp.	grated orange zest	10 mL
1/2 tsp.	salt	2 mL
1/2 cup	Olympic Natural Yogurt	125 mL
3 lb.	chicken parts, skinned	1.5 kg
2 tbsp.	oil	30 mL

Combine cornflake crumbs, sugar, cinnamon, orange zest and salt in a blender and mix until well blended. Pour mixture onto a sheet of wax paper or paper plate. Pour yogurt into a bowl. Dip chicken parts into yogurt, then coat with crumb mixture, pressing crumbs into chicken. Grease baking pan with oil, add chicken and bake at 400° F. (200°C) about 30 minutes or until tender. Makes 4 servings.

Chicken a la Sherry

Great with rice or over toast!

1 cup	mushrooms, sliced	250 mL
1	green or red pepper, chopped	1
1/4 cup	butter	60 mL
1/4 cup	flour	60 mL
1/4 cup	butter	60 mL
dash	cayenne	dash
	salt and pepper	
1-1/2 cups	chicken stock	375 mL
1 cup	Olympic Natural Yogurt	250 mL
1 tsp.	cornstarch	5 mL
1 cup	cooked chicken, cubed	250 mL
1 cup	green peas, cooked	250 mL
1/4 cup	sherry	60 mL

Saute mushrooms and peppers in butter until lightly browned and set aside. In another pan, blend butter and flour to form a roux. Add cayenne, salt and pepper and cook over low heat until bubbling. Remove from heat and add chicken stock, stirring well. Mix yogurt with cornstarch and blend gradually into the stock mixture. Bring to the boiling point, stirring constantly, about 1 minute. Add chicken, peas, and sauteed mushroom and peppers. Reheat, then add sherry just before serving. Serves 4.

Peach Flavored Chicken

Peachy Keen!

1 cup	Olympic Natural Yogurt	250 mL
2 tbsp.	peach jam	30 mL
1 tsp.	cornstarch	5 mL
1 cup	red pepper, julienne	250 mL
1/2 cup	onion, chopped	125 mL
2 tsp.	curry powder	10 mL
1/4 tsp.	salt	1 mL
1/4 tsp.	ground pepper	1 mL
3/4 cup	chicken stock	375 mL
1-1/2 lb.	chicken breasts, boned and cut in 1/2" strips	750 g
1 cup	frozen peas	250 mL
2 tsp.	lemon juice	10 mL

Combine a small amount of yogurt with peach jam and cornstarch and stir back into yogurt. Combine red pepper, onion, curry powder, salt, pepper and 1/2 cup chicken broth. Bring to a boil, then reduce heat and simmer uncovered until onion is tender (3 to 4 minutes). Stir in chicken and simmer uncovered for 2 minutes, adding more chicken broth if necessary. Add peas and continue cooking until tender, about 4 minutes. Reduce heat, stir in yogurt and stir over low heat until hot, about 2 to 3 minutes. Sprinkle with lemon juice and stir gently. Serve over steamed rice. Serves 4.

Turkey Enchiladas

Great warmed up too!

1/2 lb.	ground raw turkey (or chopped cooked turkey or chicken)	250 g
2 tbsp.	butter	30 mL
1 cup	celery, chopped	250 mL
1 cup	onion, diced	250 mL
1 cup	Olympic Natural Yogurt	250 mL
10 oz.	can Cream of Chicken soup	284 mL
4 oz.	can green chilies, chopped	125 mL
6 to 8	flour tortillas	6 to 8
1 lb.	Monterey Jack cheese, shredded	500 g

Saute the turkey in the butter until the pink has disappeared. (Omit this step if using cooked turkey or chicken). Drain and set aside. Add the celery and onion to the frying pan and cook until the onion is limp. Mix the yogurt and soup together and add chilies and turkey. Add celery and onion and mix well. Saving 1/3 of the mixture for a sauce, divide the rest of the mixture evenly among the warm tortillas, roll up and place seam side down on an oiled shallow baking pan. Add the balance of the sauce and top with the shredded cheese. Bake at 350°F. (180°C) for 30 minutes or until the cheese is melted. Serves 6 to 8.

Turkey Burgers

An excellent alternative for cholesterol watchers!

1/2 lb.	ground turkey, uncooked	250 g
1	onion, finely chopped	1
1 cup	bread crumbs	250 mL
1/4 cup	Olympic Natural Yogurt	60 mL
1/2 tsp.	salt	2 mL
	pepper	
1/2 tsp.	sage	2 mL
1 tsp.	tarragon	5 mL
2 tbsp.	parsley	30 mL
1 tbsp.	sesame seeds	15 mL

Mix all ingredients together except the sesame seeds and shape into burgers. Cover and refrigerate for at least 30 minutes. Coat the burgers with sesame seeds and barbecue until the meat is thoroughly cooked. Makes 4 burgers.

The Yogurt Dill Sauce (see Appetizers, Dips & Sauces) is a complementary, zingy accompaniment!

SALAD & DRESSINGS

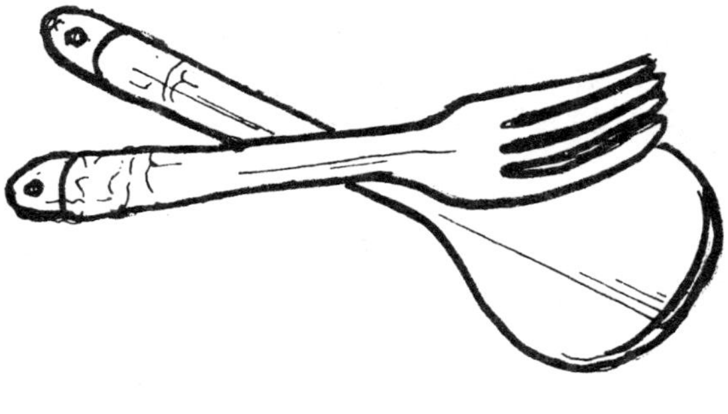

Shrimp Stuffed Avocados

Sprinkle avocados with lemon juice to prevent them from turning brown!

1 tsp.	dill weed	5 mL
1/4 cup	Olympic Natural Yogurt	60 mL
1 cup	shrimp meat	250 g
1/2 cup	cucumber, chopped, unpeeled	125 mL
1/4 cup	celery, chopped	60 mL
2 tbsp.	green onion, chopped	30 mL
3	avocados, halved and pitted	3
	lemon juice	

Combine dill weed, yogurt, shrimp, cucumber, celery and green onion. Dip cut surface of avocado halves in lemon juice. Spoon salad into avocado halves. Arrange on a platter. Serves 6.

Greek Salad

Serve with Moussaka, Souvlaki and Tzatziki (all in this book)!

6	Roma tomatoes, cut into chunks	6
1	red onion, coarsely cut	1
2	English cucumbers, cut into chunks	2
2 each	red and green peppers, cut into pieces	2
1/2 cup	olive oil	125 mL
1/3 cup	Olympic Natural Yogurt	75 mL
1 tsp.	lemon juice	5 mL
1 tsp. each	oregano and basil	5 mL each
1 clove	garlic, minced	1 clove
1/2 tsp.	salt	2 mL
	freshly ground pepper	
1 tsp.	sugar	5 mL
6 oz.	Feta cheese, coarsely crumbled	180 g
1/2 cup	Greek Kalamata olives, whole	125 mL
4 tbsp. each	fresh mint and parsley	60 mL

Toss tomatoes, onion, cucumber and peppers together. To make the dressing, combine the olive oil, yogurt, lemon juice, oregano, basil, garlic, salt, pepper and sugar together and whisk well. Pour over the salad. Top with Feta cheese, scatter olives over the salad and sprinkle with mint and parsley. Serves 6.

(From top center, clockwise)

Greek Salad, page 130
Tzatziki, page 14
Chicken Souvlaki, page 122
Moussaka, page 100

Avocado Salad with Capers

A nice tangy dressing to compliment the avocado!

1 tsp.	dry mustard powder	5 mL
1/4 tsp.	salt	1 mL
1/4 tsp.	black pepper	1 mL
1 tsp.	sugar	5 mL
1/3 cup	Olympic Natural Yogurt	75 mL
1/3 cup	mayonnaise	75 mL
1 tbsp.	capers	15 mL
2	avocados, skinned and sliced	2
	juice of half a lemon	
1 tbsp.	chives, snipped	15 mL

Mix mustard, salt, pepper, sugar, yogurt, mayonnaise and capers together and chill. Toss the avocado slices in lemon juice. Serve with dressing spooned over and sprinkle with chives. Serves 2 to 4.

Fettuccine Salad

Delicious!

1/2 cup	Olympic Natural Yogurt	125 mL
1/2 cup	olive oil	125 mL
1/4 cup	white wine vinegar	60 mL
2 tbsp.	lemon juice	30 mL
1 tsp.	Worcestershire sauce	5 mL
	Tabasco sauce	
1/2 tsp.	dry mustard powder	2 mL
1 tsp.	basil	5 mL
1 tsp.	tarragon	5 mL
1 lb.	fettuccine, cooked al dente	500 g
	OR fancy pasta such as bows	
1	red pepper, julienne	1
1	green pepper, julienne	1
2 cups	mushrooms, sliced	500 mL
1/2 lb.	shrimp	250 g
2	tomatoes, cut in wedges	2

Combine yogurt, olive oil, vinegar, lemon juice, Worcestershire sauce, Tabasco sauce, mustard powder, basil and tarragon and mix well. Set aside. Cook fettuccine and drain thoroughly. Toss fettuccine, dressing, red and green pepper strips, mushrooms and shrimp until well coated and blended. Arrange tomato wedges on top and chill 2 hours. Serves 8 to 10.

Leek and Grape Salad

Quick and impressive!

1 tsp.	Dijon mustard	5 mL
1 tsp.	salt	5 mL
	juice of 1/2 lemon	
1	clove garlic, minced	1
1/2 cup	Olympic Natural Yogurt	125 mL
1 lb.	young leeks, trimmed, washed and chopped diagonally	500 g
18	green grapes, skinned, seeded and halved	18
1 tbsp.	each chives and parsley	15 mL

Whisk the mustard, salt, lemon, garlic and yogurt together and set aside. Cook the leeks for 2 to 3 minutes so they are still crisp. Drain and rinse under cold water to retain the bright green color. Combine with the grapes and chill well. Spoon dressing over the leeks just before serving and sprinkle with the chives and parsley. Serves 4.

Romaine Toss

A simple salad packed full of flavor!

1 tbsp.	lemon juice	15 mL
1 tsp.	anchovy paste	5 mL
2 tsp.	capers, drained	10 mL
1	clove garlic, minced	1
1/4 cup	Olympic Natural Yogurt	60 mL
2 tbsp.	mayonnaise	30 mL
1	head romaine, torn into pieces	
	black olives, halved	

Combine lemon juice, paste, capers, and garlic and mix well. (Use a food processor if you wish). Add yogurt and mayonnaise and process until thoroughly mixed. Set aside. Combine lettuce and olives, add dressing and toss to coat. Serve immediately. Serves 4.

Crab Louie Salad

You may substitute canned tuna for the crab!

6-1/2 oz.	tin crab meat	200 mL
2	stalks celery, chopped	2
2	shallots, grated	2
2 tbsp.	lemon juice	30 mL
1/4 tsp.	dill weed	1 mL
	black pepper, freshly ground	
1/2 cup	Olympic Natural Yogurt	125 mL
1/2 cup	mayonnaise	125 mL
	lettuce leaves	

Drain crab meat and remove membranes. Combine with celery, shallots, lemon juice, dill weed, pepper, yogurt and mayonnaise. Toss lightly and arrange on lettuce leaves. Serves 4.

Green Bean and Mushroom Salad

A nice first course for a luncheon!

1-1/2 cups	fresh green beans, blanched	375 mL
	OR	
2-14 oz.	tins green beans	398 mL
1/2 cup	mushrooms, sliced	125 mL
1/4 cup	Olympic Natural Yogurt	60 mL
2 tbsp.	green onion	30 mL
2 tbsp.	mayonnaise	30 mL
2 tbsp.	cottage cheese	30 mL
1 tbsp.	parsley, minced	15 mL
1 tsp.	lemon juice	5 mL
1 tsp.	Dijon mustard	5 mL
	salt and lemon pepper	

Combine beans and mushrooms. In blender combine remaining ingredients and process until pureed. Pour over bean/mushroom mixture and toss to coat. Serve immediately or refrigerate until serving. Serves 3 to 4.

Hawaiian Shrimp Salad

Aloha!

2 cups	shrimp	500 mL
1/2 cup	celery, finely chopped	125 mL
14 oz.	tin pineapple chunks	398 mL
1/4 cup	red pepper, chopped	60 mL
1/4 cup	green pepper, chopped	60 mL
10 oz.	tin water chestnuts, chopped	284 mL
2	green onions, chopped	2
1/2	English cucumber, chopped	1/2
1/3 cup	sour cream	75 mL
1/3 cup	mayonnaise	75 mL
1/3 cup	Olympic Natural Yogurt	75 mL
1 tbsp.	soy sauce	15 mL
1 tbsp.	Worcestershire sauce	15 mL
1 tsp.	lemon juice	5 mL

Combine shrimp, celery, pineapple, peppers, chestnuts, green onions and cucumber. Separately, combine sour cream, mayonnaise, yogurt, soy sauce, Worcestershire sauce and lemon juice. Cover both mixtures and refrigerate for minimum of one hour to blend flavors. When ready to serve, toss shrimp mixture with yogurt mixture. Serve on a lettuce leaf. Serves 4.

Indienne Salad

A touch of curry for an exotic flavor!

8 oz.	tin crushed pineapple, drained	250 mL
7-1/2 oz.	can tuna, drained	213 g
1/4 cup	sour cream	60 mL
1/4 cup	Olympic Natural Yogurt	60 mL
1/2 cup	celery, chopped	125 mL
3	green onions, chopped	3
1/4 cup	raisins	60 mL
1 tsp.	curry powder	5 mL
2 large	tomatoes	2 large
2 large	lettuce leaves	2 large

Mix together all ingredients except tomatoes and lettuce. With stem side down, cut each tomato in half vertically and horizontally without cutting all the way through, to make 4 large wedges. Cut again between these cuts to make 8 joined wedges. Place a lettuce leaf on each salad plate, place tomatoes on leaf and gently spoon mixture into tomato "star" center and side slits. Serves 2.

Tomato and Bean Salad

This is stunning!

1 lb.	green beans, trimmed and cut into 2" lengths	500 g
24	cherry tomatoes, washed and halved	24
2	cloves garlic, minced	1
1 tbsp.	dry mustard powder	15 mL
1/2 cup	Olympic Natural Yogurt	125 mL
2 tbsp.	lemon juice	30 mL
1 tsp.	sugar	5 mL
1/4 tsp.	pepper	1 mL
1/4 tsp.	salt	1 mL

Steam beans about 5 minutes and plunge into a bowl of ice water to stop the cooking and set the color. Place in bowl and combine with the tomatoes. Whisk remaining ingredients together until smooth. Toss the dressing with the beans and tomatoes and serve immediately. Serves 6.

Note: For an even more colorful look use half red and half yellow cherry tomatoes.

Potato Salad

Very delicious and moist!

6	potatoes, cooked and cubed	6
6	eggs, boiled, peeled and sliced	6
4	green onions, chopped	4
8	radishes, sliced	8
1/2 cup	Olympic Natural Yogurt	125 mL
1/2 cup	mayonnaise	125 mL
	salt and pepper	
	dill and paprika	

Combine all ingredients except dill and paprika and mix well, saving some egg slices and radishes for garnish. Sprinkle with dill and/or paprika if desired. Refrigerate before serving. Serves 8.

Cantonese Chicken Salad

Lots of good crunchy things in this salad!

3 tbsp.	dark sesame oil	45 mL
2	chicken breasts, cooked and diced	2
1/4 lb.	snow peas	125 g
2	carrots, peeled and julienned	2
2	celery stocks, julienned	2
1 cup	jicama, peeled and julienned	250 mL
1	green pepper, julienned	1
1	green onion, finely chopped	1
1/4 lb.	mushrooms, sliced	125 g
8 oz.	can water chestnuts, sliced	227 mL
8 oz.	can bamboo shoots	227 mL
1/3 cup	rice wine vinegar	75 mL
1/3 cup	soy sauce	75 mL
1/3 cup	Olympic Natural Yogurt	75 mL
2 tbsp.	sugar	30 mL
3 tbsp.	ginger, freshly grated	45 mL
	ground white pepper	
	slivered almonds, sunflower seeds, OR pine nuts	

Heat the sesame oil in a wok and stir fry the chicken for 2 minutes or until cooked through. Combine the chicken with the rest of the ingredients from the snow peas to the bamboo shoots and mix well. For the dressing, combine the rice vinegar, soy sauce, yogurt, sugar, ginger and pepper in a blender. Pour over rest of ingredients and chill for at least an hour. Sprinkle with nuts if desired. Serves 8.

Spinach Salad

Light and refreshing!

1 lb.	fresh spinach, washed	500 g
1/2 lb.	large mushrooms, sliced	250 g
2	eggs, hard cooked and grated	2
2	green onions, sliced	2
4 slices	bacon, fried crisp and crumbled	4 slices
1	red onion, sliced thinly	1
1/4 cup	mayonnaise	60 mL
1/4 cup	Olympic Natural Yogurt	60 mL
1 tbsp.	red wine vinegar	15 mL
2	cloves garlic, minced	2
	salt and pepper	
	croutons	

Tear spinach into bite-sized pieces. Toss with mushrooms, eggs, green onions, bacon and red onion. To make the dressing, combine mayonnaise, yogurt, wine vinegar, garlic, salt and pepper, mixing well. Make dressing several hours ahead and store in refrigerator to blend flavors. At serving time, pour over salad and toss. Add croutons if desired. Serves 3 to 4.

Waldorf Salad

Green grapes add color and a nice texture!

	lettuce leaves	
1/4 cup	walnuts, chopped	60 mL
1/4 cup	raisins	60 mL
1 tbsp.	sunflower seeds	15 mL
1 stalk	celery, chopped	1 stalk
3	apples, peeled and chopped	3
1 tbsp.	honey	30 mL
1 tbsp.	wine vinegar	15 mL
1/2 cup	Olympic Natural Yogurt	125 mL

Line a salad bowl (or individual bowls) with the lettuce leaves. Mix walnuts, raisins, sunflower seeds, celery and apples together. Add the honey and wine vinegar to the yogurt, mix well and pour over the fruit and nut mixture. Serve in the lettuce leaves. Serves 4.

Melon & Prawn Salad

Serve in cantaloupe halves!

3/4 cup	mayonnaise	185 mL
3/4 cup	Olympic Natural Yogurt	185 mL
2 tbsp.	lime juice	30 mL
1/4 cup	mango chutney, finely chopped	60 mL
1 tbsp.	curry powder	15 mL
1 large	honeydew melon	1 large
1 lb.	prawns, cooked	500 g
2	cantaloupe, quartered and seeded	2
	mint leaves	

Combine mayonnaise, yogurt, lime juice, chutney and curry powder. Chill. Discard seeds from melon and scoop out balls using a melon baller. Add melon balls and prawns to dressing and toss gently. Remove the seeds from the cantaloupe, quarter and gently spoon in the prawn and melon mixture. Top with fresh mint leaves. Serves 8.

Curried Rice Salad

The fruit adds a nice contrast in flavor and texture to the rice!

3 cups	white rice cooked and cooled	750 mL
1/2 tsp.	salt	2 mL
3/4 cup	Olympic Natural Yogurt	185 mL
1/4 cup	mayonnaise	60 mL
1/4 cup	orange juice concentrate, thawed	60 mL
1 tsp.	curry powder	5 mL
1 large	orange, peeled and sectioned	1 large
1	banana, thinly sliced	1
1/2 cup	raisins	125 mL
1/2 cup	celery, chopped	125 mL
1/4 cup	nuts, chopped	60 mL

Combine rice, salt, yogurt, mayonnaise, orange juice concentrate and curry powder and mix well. Add orange, banana, raisins, celery and nuts and toss to mix. Garnish with additional orange and banana slices and serve chilled. Serves 6 to 8.

Bacon and Egg Salad

You'll know why it's called this after you make it!

2 tbsp.	Olympic Natural Yogurt	30 mL
1 tbsp.	grated orange zest	15 mL
	juice of one orange	
1 tsp.	vinegar	5 mL
1 tsp.	salt	5 mL
1/2 tsp.	pepper	2 mL
1 clove	garlic, minced	1 clove
3/4 cup	olive oil	185 mL
1 head	lettuce, broken into bite sized pieces	1 head
1/2 cup	bacon, cooked and crumbled	125 mL
14 oz.	tin peaches, halved	398 mL

Mix yogurt, orange zest, orange juice, vinegar, salt, pepper, garlic and oil in a blender. Put the lettuce in a salad bowl, add the dressing and toss well. Top with bacon and peach halves (rounded side up).

Marinated Bean Salad

Use all the different beans from your garden!

14 oz.	tin garbanzo beans, drained	398 mL
14 oz.	tin kidney beans, drained	398 mL
14 oz.	tin wax beans	398 mL
14 oz.	tin green beans	398 mL
1	red onion, sliced	1
1 cup	cucumber, chopped	250 mL
3	celery stalks, chopped	3
3/4 cup	Olympic Natural Yogurt	185 mL
1 tsp.	lemon juice	5 mL
2 tsp.	cumin	10 mL
2 cloves	garlic, crushed	2 cloves
1/2 tsp.	dry mustard powder	2 mL
1/2 tsp.	tarragon	2 mL
	salt and pepper	
1/4 cup	parsley, finely chopped	60 mL

Drain beans and add cucumber and celery. Combine yogurt, lemon juice, cumin, garlic, mustard, tarragon, salt and pepper and toss with bean mixture. Sprinkle with parsley. Serves 12.

Caesar Salad

Thank goodness for Julius!

2 or 3	anchovy fillets	2 or 3
3 cloves	garlic	3 cloves
2 tbsp.	red wine vinegar	30 mL
1/4 cup	olive oil	60 mL
1/4 cup	Olympic Natural Yogurt	60 mL
2 tsp.	Dijon mustard	10 mL
dash	Tabasco sauce	dash
1 tbsp.	lemon juice	15 mL
1 tsp.	Worcestershire Sauce	5 mL
1/4 cup	Parmesan cheese, freshly grated	60 mL
	croutons	
	Romaine lettuce, broken into bite sized pieces	

Combine all ingredients except Parmesan, croutons and Romaine in a blender. Pour over Romaine and toss along with cheese and croutons. Serves 4.

Caribbean Shrimp and Papaya Salad

This must have originated in Heaven!

1/2 lb.	shrimp meat	250 g
1/4 cup	chili sauce	60 mL
2	green onions, chopped	2
1/4 tsp.	cinnamon	1 mL
dash	Tabasco sauce	dash
1 large	ripe papaya	1 large
1	star fruit	1
	lettuce leaves	
1/2 cup	coconut	125 mL
	green onions	

Combine shrimp, chili sauce, green onions, cinnamon and Tabasco sauce. Cover and let stand. Half the papaya and scoop out the seeds and pulp. Lightly score the papaya halves with a sharp knife to make an "X". Slice the star fruit crosswise into 1/4" slices. Line salad plates with the lettuce leaves and sprinkle with coconut. Place a papaya half on each plate and spoon the shrimp mixture inside the halves. Garnish the lettuce leaves with the star fruit, and green onions. Serves 2.

Louis Salad

Salad fit for a "King"!

1/2 cup	onion, diced	125 mL
1/2 cup	celery, diced	125 mL
1/2 cup	carrot, diced	125 mL
4 slices	lemon	4 slices
	salt and pepper	
1 cup	water	250 mL
8 oz.	fish filets	250 g
2 tbsp.	green onion, chopped	30 mL
2 tbsp.	chili sauce	30 mL
1 tbsp.	mayonnaise	15 mL
1 tbsp.	Olympic Natural Yogurt	15 mL
1 tbsp.	lemon juice	15 mL
	lettuce leaves	

Combine onion, celery, carrot, lemon slices, salt and pepper in a skillet. Add water and bring to a boil. Add fish, spoon vegetables over fish and return to a boil. Reduce heat, cover and let simmer until fish flakes easily, about 5 minutes. Remove fish, discarding liquid and vegetables. Cool, then cover and refrigerate until chilled. Combine remaining ingredients except lettuce, mix well and chill. Cut fish into bite-sized pieces and serve on lettuce leaves. Spoon sauce over fish. Serves 2.

Pear and Feta Salad

This lunch dish will satisfy all your dessert cravings!

1	ripe pear	1
	(D'Anjou, Comice or Bartlett)	
2 tbsp.	lemon juice	30 mL
1 head	lettuce, cleaned and dried	1 head
2 tbsp.	walnut oil	30 mL
1/2 cup	walnuts, chopped and toasted	125 mL
1/2 cup	Feta cheese, crumbled	125 mL
2 tsp.	red wine vinegar	10 mL
	freshly ground pepper	

Slice the pear thinly and cover with lemon juice. Break the lettuce into bite-sized pieces, drizzle with oil and toss. Gently add the walnuts and feta, sprinkle in the vinegar and grate in the pepper. Toss to distribute. Arrange the pear slices on top of the salad and serve. Yield 4 to 5 servings.

Chicken Mousse

Chill in individual molds and serve in lettuce cups or use one large salad mold!

2 tbsp.	unflavored gelatin	30 mL
1/2 cup	cold water	125 mL
2 cups	boiling water	500 mL
3	chicken bouillon cubes	3
3 tbsp.	lemon juice	45 mL
1 tsp.	dry mustard powder	5 mL
2 tsp.	curry powder	10 mL
1/2 tsp.	salt	2 mL
2 cups	Olympic Natural Yogurt	500 mL
3 cups	chicken, cooked and cubed	750 mL
1/4 cup	green onions, chopped	60 mL
1 cup	celery, finely chopped	250 mL
1/4 cup	green pepper, finely chopped	60 mL
1/4 cup	almonds, toasted and chopped	60 mL
	lettuce or watercress	

Sprinkle gelatin over 1/2 cup cold water and let stand 5 minutes to soften. In a large bowl, pour boiling water over bouillon cubes and stir to dissolve. Add gelatin, lemon juice, mustard, curry powder and salt and stir until gelatin is dissolved. Stir in yogurt, mixing well. Refrigerate until consistency of unbeaten egg whites, about 30 to 45 minutes. Fold in chicken, onion, celery, green pepper and almonds and pour into 8 to 10 individual oiled molds or 1-1/2 quart mold. Refrigerate until firm, about 4 hours or overnight. Unmold onto lettuce or garnish with watercress. Serves 8 to 10.

Creamy Coleslaw

Add a sprinkle of celery or caraway seed!

1	small head cabbage, shredded or thinly sliced	1
1/2	red cabbage shredded	1/2
1	apple, grated	1
2	carrots, grated	2
1/4 cup	onion, chopped	60 mL
1	red or green pepper, diced	1
1/4 cup	mayonnaise	60 mL
1/4 cup	Olympic Natural Yogurt	60 mL
2 tbsp.	sour cream	30 mL
1 tbsp.	sugar	15 mL
1 tsp.	lemon juice	5 mL
1/2 tsp.	salt	2 mL
	pepper, freshly ground	

Prepare cabbage, apple, carrots, onion and pepper and mix lightly. Combine mayonnaise, yogurt and sour cream, along with sugar, lemon juice, salt and pepper and mix well. Pour over cabbage mixture and toss lightly. Serves 6.

Ranch Dressing

Serve with your favorite lettuce!

3/4 cup	Olympic Natural Yogurt	185 mL
1/2 cup	light mayonnaise	125 mL
2 tbsp.	tarragon vinegar	30 mL
1 tbsp.	onion, minced	15 mL
2 tsp.	parsley, minced	10 mL
1/4 tsp.	celery seed	1 mL
1/4 tsp.	Dijon mustard	1 mL
1/2 tsp.	garlic powder	2 mL

Whip all ingredients together and chill. Makes 1-1/4 cups (300 mL).

Thousand Island Dressing

You'll never buy dressing again!

2 tbsp.	chili sauce	30 mL
1 tbsp.	onion, finely chopped	15 mL
1 tbsp.	green pepper, finely chopped	15 mL
1	egg, hard boiled and chopped	1
1 tbsp.	dill pickle, chopped	15 mL
1/2 tsp.	lemon juice	2 mL
1/2 tsp.	prepared mustard	2 mL
1/4 tsp.	salt	1 mL
1/2 cup	Olympic Natural Yogurt	125 mL

Combine all ingredients and refrigerate. Makes about 1 cup (250 mL).

Poppy Seed Dressing

The poppy seeds give it crunch and the grenadine gives it color!

1/2 cup	Olympic Natural Yogurt	125 mL
2 tsp.	grenadine	10 mL
1 tsp.	poppy seeds	5 mL

Combine, chill and serve! Makes 1/2 cup (125 mL).

Add Olympic Natural Yogurt to your favorite bottled dressing for a creamier salad topping!

Yogurt Mayonnaise

Keeps for at least a week in the fridge!

4	egg yolks	4
1/2 tsp.	dry powdered mustard	2 mL
	salt to taste	
	ground black pepper, to taste	
1 tsp.	lemon juice	5 mL
1-1/4 cup	olive oil	300 mL
1-1/4 cup	Olympic Natural Yogurt	300 mL

Whisk egg yolks, mustard, salt and pepper together until smooth. Add lemon juice and beat until smooth again. Add the olive oil, a small amount at a time, beating in each addition. When 1/4 of the oil has been added, add the remainder in a steady stream. If the sauce becomes too thick before all the oil has been added, thin it down a little by beating in a small amount of the yogurt. Beat in the yogurt, a tablespoon at a time. Adjust the seasoning to taste. Cover the bowl and chill thoroughly before serving. Makes about 2 cups (500 mL).

Bleu Cheese Dressing

The same sharp taste with a fraction of the calories!

1 cup	Olympic Natural Yogurt	250 mL
1/2 cup	blue cheese, crumbled	125 mL
1 clove	garlic, minced	1 clove
pinch	dry mustard	pinch
1 tsp.	lemon juice	5 mL
1/4 tsp.	grated lemon zest	1 mL
1 tsp.	chives, chopped	5 mL
1 tsp.	parsley, chopped	5 mL
1 tsp.	basil, chopped	5 mL

Puree ingredients in a blender until smooth. Makes about 2 cups (500 mL).

Cucumber Dressing

If using an English cucumber, it is not necessary to peel before grating!

1 cup	Olympic Natural Yogurt	250 mL
1 large	cucumber, peeled and chopped	1 large
1 clove	garlic, minced	1 clove
1 tsp.	lemon juice or red wine vinegar	5 mL
1/4 tsp.	paprika	1 mL
2 tbsp.	green onion, finely chopped	30 mL

Blend all ingredients and refrigerate for several hours to blend flavors. Makes about 1-1/2 cups (375 mL).

Honey Yogurt Dressing

Good cold over Romaine and hot over broccoli!

1 cup	Olympic Natural Yogurt	250 mL
2 tbsp.	lemon juice	30 mL
2 tbsp.	honey	30 mL
2 tbsp.	mayonnaise	30 mL
1 tsp.	horseradish	5 mL
1 tsp.	Dijon mustard	5 mL
	almond chips, toasted	

Mix all ingredients together and use as desired, hot or cold. Makes about 1-1/2 cups (375 mL).

Avocado Dressing

A nice, delicate dressing!

1/2 cup	Olympic Natural Yogurt	125 mL
1	ripe avocado	1
1/4 cup	dry white wine	60 mL
1 tbsp.	onion, minced	15 mL
2 tbsp.	lemon or lime juice	30 mL
	salt	
1/2 tsp.	ground cumin	2 mL
1/4 tsp.	cayenne pepper	1 mL

Peel avocado and mash with a fork. Blend in remaining ingredients and mix until smooth. Makes about 1 cup (250 mL).

Tangy Yogurt Dressing

This is a good basic dressing. You can add herbs and spices to change the flavor!

1 cup	Olympic Natural Yogurt	250 mL
1 tsp.	sugar	5 mL
1 tsp.	white vinegar	5 mL
1 clove	garlic, minced	1 clove
1 tsp.	Worcestershire sauce	5 mL
1 tsp.	tarragon	5 mL
1 tsp.	dry mustard	5 mL
1/2 tsp.	salt	2 mL
1/4 tsp.	pepper	1 mL

Combine ingredients and stir until smooth. Makes about 1 cup (250 mL).

SOUP

Pea Soup

The addition of yogurt and sherry just before serving gives a distinct pleasant flavor!

1 lb.	dried green split peas	500 g
5 cups	chicken stock	1.2 L
5 cups	water	1.2 L
	OR	
1	meaty ham bone	1
2	smoked ham hocks	2
2	ribs celery, leaves included, diced	2
3 tbsp.	parsley, chopped	45 mL
1/2 tsp.	dried tarragon	2 mL
1/4 cup	butter	60 mL
1 cup	carrots, diced	250 mL
1 cup	onion, diced	250 mL
2 tbsp.	dry sherry	30 mL
1/2 cup	Olympic Natural Yogurt	125 mL
1/2 tsp.	pepper, freshly ground	2 mL

Rinse peas and combine with stock and water and bring to a boil. Add ham bone, celery, half the parsley and the tarragon. Reduce heat to medium-low and simmer, partially covered, stirring occasionally for 45 minutes. Melt butter cook carrots and onion about 10 minutes. Add to soup pot and simmer 30 minutes, partially covered. Remove soup from the heat and remove meat from the bone and add to soup. Add sherry, yogurt, pepper and remaining parsley and heat through. Serve immediately. Serves 6.

Substitute Olympic Natural Yogurt for milk in canned soups!

Corn Chowder

One of my Mom's specialties!

1	onion, chopped	1
3	potatoes, peeled and diced	3
12 oz.	can whole kernel corn	341 mL
1-1/2 cups	milk	375 mL
5	slices bacon	5
1 tsp.	cornstarch	5 mL
1/4 cup	Olympic Natural Yogurt	60 mL
	salt and pepper	

Fry onion and add to potatoes. Add water and cook until tender. Do not discard potato water. Add corn and milk and heat to boiling point. Fry bacon and add to liquid. Add cornstarch to yogurt and mix well. Gradually add soup to yogurt, one tablespoon at a time up to 1/2 cup, stirring continuously. Add yogurt gradually back to corn chowder, season with salt and pepper and serve immediately. Serves 4.

Borscht

Excellent served chilled on a hot day!

2 cups	beets, shredded	500 mL
1 cup	carrots, shredded	250 mL
1 cup	onion, chopped finely	250 mL
2 cups	brown stock	500 mL
1 cup	cabbage, shredded	250 mL
1/4 cup	lemon juice	50 mL
2 tbsp.	horseradish	30 mL
1 dollop	Olympic Natural Yogurt	1 dollop
	dill	

Cook beets and when cool enough to handle, slip off skins and shred. Cook carrots and onion in boiling salted water (2-2/3 cups or 675 mL) for 20 minutes and add beets. Add stock, cabbage, lemon juice and horseradish and cook uncovered 15 minutes. Serve hot or chilled with a dollop of yogurt and a sprinkle of dill for garnish. Serves 4.

Bean Soup

This may replace your childhood "comfort food"!

5 cups	cooked beans, Pinto, black, etc.	1.2 L
16 cups	water	4 L
2 tbsp.	salt	30 mL
3 cups	canned tomatoes	750 mL
1 cup	onions, chopped	250 mL
6	cloves garlic, minced	6
1 cup	olive oil or butter	250 mL
1 cup	Olympic Natural Yogurt	250 mL
6	potatoes, quartered	6
1 cup	carrots, diced	250 mL
1 cup	celery, diced	250 mL
2 cups	potatoes, diced	500 mL
3	green onions, diced	3
1 tsp.	black pepper	5 mL

Soak 2-1/2 cups (625 mL) dry beans overnight. (This will yield 5 cups when cooked.) Bring to a boil, add salt and simmer until tender. Put tomatoes, onions, garlic and 1/2 cup (125 mL) olive oil in frying pan and simmer 10 minutes. Add quartered potatoes to beans and cook until done. Remove potatoes, mash with remaining olive oil and yogurt and add to tomato mixture. Put aside. To bean pot add carrots and celery and simmer until almost tender. Add diced potatoes and simmer 5 minutes. Add potato/tomato/onion mixture, green onions and black pepper and bring to a boil. Remove from heat and serve immediately. Serves a large family.

Chicken Noodle Yogurt Soup

A great warm-up on chilly days!

1 tbsp.	olive oil	15 mL
1	large onion, finely chopped	1
1 tsp.	thyme	5 mL
1 tsp.	dill	5 mL
1/2 tsp.	pepper	2 mL
3	cloves garlic, minced	3
5	sprigs parsley	5
3	carrots, thinly sliced	3
4 cups	chicken broth	1 L
4 oz.	medium wide egg noddles	125 g
2 cups	cooked turkey or chicken, cubed	500 mL
1 cup	Olympic Natural Yogurt	250 mL
1 tbsp.	cornstarch	15 mL
6	green onions, chopped	6

Heat oil and add chopped onion, thyme, dill, and pepper. Cook, stirring often, for approximately 8 minutes. Stir in garlic, add parsley, carrots and broth and bring to a boil. Reduce heat, cover and boil gently until carrots are tender (about 15 minutes). Discard parsley, increase heat to high and add noodles. Cook uncovered until noodles are cooked al dente (approx. 8 minutes). Add chicken. In another bowl, blend yogurt and cornstarch until smooth. Gradually blend in about 1 cup of hot broth mixture, then stir broth-yogurt mixture back into soup and heat until hot. Garnish with green onions. Serves 6.

Spinach Soup

This version is popular in the Middle East!

1/2 lb.	spinach, finely chopped*	250 g
2	onions, finely chopped	2
2	cloves garlic, minced	2
1 tsp.	cumin	5 mL
1/2 tsp.	tumeric	2 mL
dash	cinnamon	dash
dash	cayenne	dash
1/4 cup	butter	60 mL
4 cups	chicken stock	1 L
1-1/2 cups	Olympic Natural Yogurt	375 mL
1 cup	cooked rice	250 mL
	salt and pepper	
1 tsp.	dill	5 mL

Wash and dry spinach. Saute onions, garlic, cumin, tumeric, cinnamon and cayenne in butter until the onions are translucent. Increase heat, add chicken stock and bring to a boil. Add spinach and simmer 1 minute. Remove from heat and set aside. When cool, combine stock and spinach mixture and 1 cup yogurt in blender and puree. Return soup to saucepan along with rice and reheat briefly. Add salt and pepper to taste. Serve with a dollop of yogurt and sprinkle with dill. Serves 6.

*Substitute one 10 oz. package frozen spinach (defrosted) if you prefer!

Carrot Soup

You can individualize to your taste by adding your favorite seeds, nuts and herbs!

2 lb.	carrots, sliced	1 kg
4 cups	stock	1 L
1	potato, cubed	1
1/4 cup	olive oil or butter	60 mL
1 cup	onion, chopped	250 mL
2	cloves garlic, crushed	2
1 tsp.	curry powder	5 mL
1/3 cup	seeds (pumpkin, sunflower, etc.) OR nuts (peanuts, cashews, almonds)	75 mL
1 cup	Olympic Natural Yogurt	250 mL
2 tbsp.	sherry	30 mL

Combine carrots, stock and potato and bring to a boil. Simmer, covered for 15 minutes. Let cool to room temperature. Saute onion, garlic, curry and seeds in butter. Combine with carrot mixture and yogurt, puree in blender until smooth. Return to a double boiler and heat until just hot. Add sherry and garnish with your "fave" herbs! Serves 4 to 6.

Guacamole Soup

Ole!

2	avocados, chopped	2
1/2	dried chili pepper, crushed	1/2
1/3 cup	onion, chopped	75 mL
3 cups	chicken stock	750 mL
1 cup	Olympic Natural Yogurt	250 mL
1 tsp.	salt	5 mL
dash	cayenne pepper	dash
1 tbsp.	parsley	15 mL
1/2 tsp.	Tabasco sauce	2 mL
1	avocado, cubed	1
2	corn tortillas, for garnish	2

In a blender, whirl at low speed the avocados, chili pepper, onion and stock. When smooth, heat on top of double boiler to boiling point. Add yogurt, mix well and heat again to a slow simmer. Just before serving add salt, cayenne, parsley, Tabasco sauce and avocado cubes. Garnish with tortillas. Serves 4.

Mushroom and Leek Soup

We got excellent raves on this one!

1/4 cup	butter	60 mL
1	leek	1
1	clove garlic, finely chopped	1
1	carrot, finely chopped	1
1 lb.	mushrooms, sliced	500 g
3 tbsp.	flour	45 mL
1/2 tsp.	salt	2 mL
1/4 tsp.	freshly ground black pepper	1 mL
1/4 tsp.	thyme	1 mL
4 cups	chicken stock	1 L
1-1/2 cups	Olympic Natural Yogurt	375 mL
2 tbsp.	parsley, chopped	30 mL

Melt half the butter and saute the leek, garlic and carrot until tender. Add mushrooms and remaining butter and cook an additional 3 minutes. Sprinkle the flour, salt, pepper and thyme into the pan and cook, stirring one minute. Stir in stock, cover and bring to a boil. Simmer 30 minutes. Mix the yogurt with a little of the soup, return all to the skillet and reheat but do not boil. Stir in the parsley and Voila! Serves 4 to 6.

Combine Olympic Natural Yogurt with dillweed for a topping on borscht!

Broccoli Soup

Anyone for "tree" soup?

1 cup	onion, diced	250 mL
1 tbsp.	butter	15 mL
5 cups	chicken stock	1.2 L
1-1/2 lb.	broccoli, cut into florets	750 g
1-1/2 tsp.	curry powder	7 mL
1	bay leaf	1
1 tsp.	basil	5 mL
1/2 tsp.	sugar	2 mL
pinch	cayenne	pinch
2 cups	Olympic Natural Yogurt	500 mL
1/4 tsp.	nutmeg	1 mL
	black pepper, freshly ground	

Cook onions in butter until transparent. Bring stock to a boil, add broccoli and boil gently for 7 minutes or just until tender. Add onion mixture, curry, bay leaf, basil, sugar and cayenne to broccoli and simmer, partially covered for 10 to 15 minutes. Gradually add mixture to yogurt stirring vigorously, then add yogurt mixture back to soup. Heat just until hot. Do not boil. Add nutmeg and pepper. Serve immediately. Serves 4 to 6.

Norwegian Yogurt Soup

You don't have to be Scandinavian to enjoy this soup!

1 cup	Olympic Natural Yogurt	250 mL
1/2 cup	sour cream	125 mL
	salt and pepper	
1 tbsp.	dill, chopped	15 mL
1 tbsp.	brandy	15 mL
1/2 lb.	crab meat	250 g

Combine yogurt, sour cream, salt and pepper and beat until foamy. Reserve some of the dill for garnish and add the rest to the liquid. Add brandy and crab meat. Let sit in refrigerator for at least 1/2 hour until chilled well. Season to taste and garnish with dill. Makes 6 servings.

Hungarian Goulash Soup

The real thing!

2 lb.	boneless chuck, cut in 3/4" cubes	1 kg
3/4 cup	vinegar*	200 mL
6-3/4 cups	water	1.5 L
1/4 cup	olive oil	60 mL
2	onions, finely chopped	2
3	cloves garlic, minced	3
5-1/2 oz.	tin tomato paste	156 mL
28 oz.	tin tomatoes	796 mL
4	carrots, sliced	4
2	potatoes, peeled and cubed	2
2	stalks celery, chopped	2
12	whole allspice berries	12
1/4 cup	paprika	60 mL
1 tbsp.	salt	15 mL
1 tsp.	coriander	5 mL
1 tsp.	caraway seeds	5 mL
1/8 tsp.	coarse black pepper	.5 mL
1 tsp.	cornstarch	5 mL
1 cup	Olympic Natural Yogurt	250 mL

Marinate meat in vinegar and 3/4 cup (175 mL) of the water at least two hours or overnight. Heat oil over low heat, add onions and garlic and cook until the onions are limp. Add meat and marinade to onion mixture and cook until the meat is no longer pink. Stir in remaining ingredients, including remaining water. Cover and cook over low heat 2 hours. Add cornstarch to the yogurt and mix well. Add some of the hot liquid to the yogurt. Gradually add the yogurt back into the soup stirring continuously. Leave lid off and continue cooking until soup thickens. Serves 6.

* Try a flavored vinegar such as Tarragon Wine Vinegar for an unsurpassed taste your friends will try to imitate.

Hungarian Goulash Soup, page 160

Vichyssoise

The soup section wouldn't be complete without it!

3	leeks, including 2" of green, sliced	
1 stalk	celery, chopped	1 stalk
1	onion, chopped	1
1/4 cup	butter or oil	60 mL
3	potatoes, peeled and diced	3
2 cups	chicken stock	500 mL
	salt and pepper	
1 cup	Olympic Natural Yogurt	250 mL
2 tsp.	lemon juice	10 mL
1/4 cup	chives, snipped	60 mL

Saute leeks, celery and onion in butter 6 to 8 minutes or until tender but not browned. Add the potatoes, chicken stock, salt and pepper and bring to a boil. Simmer for 20 minutes or so, until the potatoes are done. Remove from heat. When cool, puree. Refrigerate at least two hours. Just before serving add the yogurt and lemon juice, ladle into chilled bowls and garnish with chives. Serves 4.

Cool as a Cuke Soup

Toss in a handful of unsalted peanuts while processing!

4	English cucumbers, quartered	4
3 cloves	garlic, peeled	3 cloves
1-1/2 cups	chicken stock	375 mL
2 cups	Olympic Natural Yogurt	500 mL
2 tbsp.	lime juice	30 mL
	salt and pepper	
1 tbsp.	freshly chopped dill	15 mL
1 tbsp.	freshly chopped parsley	15 mL
1	red pepper, diced	1

In a food processor, coarsely chop cucumbers and garlic. Add chicken stock, yogurt, and lime juice and process just to combine. Add salt and pepper. Cover and refrigerate until serving time. Garnish with dill, parsley and red pepper. Serves 6.

Chilled Zucchini Soup

Another use for all that zucchini in your garden!

1	medium zucchini, coarsely chopped	1
1	onion, chopped	1
1 clove	garlic, minced	1 clove
2 tbsp.	oil	30 mL
1 tsp.	curry powder	5 mL
1-1/2 cups	chicken stock	375 mL
1-1/2 cups	Olympic Natural Yogurt	375 mL
1 tsp.	lemon juice	5 mL
	salt and pepper	
	fresh parsley and dill, for garnish	

Saute zucchini, onion and garlic in oil until tender. Sprinkle with curry powder. Transfer to a heavy saucepan, add chicken stock and let simmer about 30 minutes, covered. Pour mixture into blender and puree. Add yogurt, lemon juice, salt and pepper and blend thoroughly. Chill for several hours before serving and garnish with fresh herbs. Serves 4.

VEGETABLES

Curried Carrots

A favorite with curry lovers!

2 cups	thinly sliced carrots	500 mL
3 tbsp.	butter	45 mL
1	clove garlic, chopped	1
2 tsp.	curry powder	10 mL
dash	Tabasco Sauce	dash
1 tbsp.	flour	15 mL
1 cup	Olympic Natural Yogurt	250 mL

Cook carrots in salted water. Drain and set aside. Heat butter, garlic, curry and Tabasco in a saucepan and stir until well blended. Add to carrots. Mix flour and yogurt until smooth and add to carrot mixture. Simmer over low heat 10 minutes. Serves 4.

Corn Fritters

We always loved these when we were kids!

2	eggs (separated)	2 eggs
1/3 cup	water	75 mL
1/3 cup	milk	75 mL
1 tbsp.	lemon juice	15 mL
1 tbsp.	olive oil	15 mL
1 cup	flour	250 mL
1/2 tsp.	salt	2 mL
1 tbsp.	sugar	15 mL
1/8 tsp.	salt	5 mL
1/2 cup	Olympic Natural Yogurt	125 mL
12 oz.	whole kernel corn	341 mL
	peanut oil	

Beat egg yolks, water and milk. Add lemon juice and olive oil and beat well. Sift flour. salt, and sugar. Combine dry and liquid ingredients in a few swift strokes. Add 1/8 tsp. (5 mL) salt to egg whites and beat until stiff. Add yogurt, drained corn and fold into batter. Drop mixture by spoonfuls into 4" peanut oil heated to 375° F. (190°C). Cook until browned on one side. Turn and brown on other side. Drain. Makes approximately 2 dozen.

Leeks with Cheese Sauce

A nice change from peas and carrots!

3 - 4	leeks	3 - 4
1/4 tsp.	salt	1 mL
1 tbsp.	lemon juice	15 mL
1/2 cup	butter	125 mL
1	onion	1
dash	garlic salt	dash
dash	cayenne	dash
1-1/2 cups	Olympic Natural Yogurt	375 mL
1	egg	1
1/2 cup	dry bread crumbs	125 mL
1/2 cup	Monterey Jack cheese	125 mL

Clean leeks well and discard the outer leaves. Trim green ends and cut in 2" pieces. Put in saucepan with water, add salt and lemon juice, cook 15 minutes. Remove from heat and drain. Melt butter in skillet, saute leaks for two minutes. Add onion and cook for one minute. Arrange mixture in shallow baking dish, sprinkle with garlic salt and cayenne. Beat yogurt and egg, pour over leeks. Sprinkle with bread crumbs and top with grated cheese. Broil until cheese is evenly browned. Serves 4.

Mushroom Stuffed Tomatoes

Serve as a main course for lunch or as a dinner vegetable!

6	tomatoes	6
2 cups	mushrooms	500 mL
3	green onions chopped	3
1 tbsp.	olive oil	15 mL
1 tsp.	salt	5 mL
1/4 tsp.	pepper	1 mL
1/2 tsp.	tarragon	2 mL
1	egg, lightly beaten	1
1/4 cup	Olympic Natural Yogurt	60 mL

Cut out stem end of tomatoes. Scoop out pulp and invert. In a skillet, saute mushrooms and green onions in olive oil for three or four minutes. Stir in salt, pepper and tarragon. Combine egg and yogurt and add to mushroom mixture. Fill shells with the mixture and place in a shallow baking pan. Bake at 400° F. (200°C) for fifteen minutes. Serves 6.

Note: As a variation, try stuffing green peppers.

Mushroom Curry

Great over wild rice!

1 lb.	fresh mushrooms	500 mL
1/4 cup	butter	60 mL
1	onion, chopped fine	1
1 tbsp.	curry powder	15 mL
1	apple, chopped	1
1/2 tsp.	salt	2 mL
1/4 tsp.	pepper	1 mL
2-1/2 cups	Olympic Natural Yogurt	625 mL
1/2 tsp.	paprika	2 mL

Leave caps of mushrooms whole and chop the stems. Melt butter in skillet, saute mushroom caps until they are lightly browned and have absorbed most of the butter (5 minutes). Remove to small bowl and set aside. Add onion and curry powder to pan and saute until onion is transparent. Add the chopped apple, chopped mushroom stems and salt and pepper. Cook until mushrooms are tender. Remove from heat, stir in yogurt and paprika. Return to heat to warm and add mushroom caps. Serve over rice. Serves 4.

Fried Cauliflowerand Garlic Yogurt Sauce

Dazzle your guests with this recipe!

1/2 cup	sour cream	125 mL
1 cup	Olympic Natural Yogurt	250 ml
1	clove garlic, crushed	1
1/4 tsp.	salt	1 mL
1	cauliflower	1
1	egg	1
pinch	salt	pinch
	peanut oil	

To make sauce - Mix sour cream, yogurt, garlic and salt until well blended. Chill until ready to serve. Separate cauliflower into florets and cook in 1/2 cup (125 mL) boiling water until almost tender (8 minutes). Drain and dry. Heat peanut oil in skillet. Beat egg and add a pinch of salt. Dip florets into the egg mixture a few at a time and deep fry until golden brown on all sides. Drain and serve with yogurt sauce. Serves only four (because they'll all want lots).

Vegetarian Kebabs

Enjoy while waiting for Bar-B-Que weather!

4	slices stale bread	4
1	green pepper	1
1/2 lb.	sharp cheese	250 g
1/2 lb.	cherry tomatoes	250 g
2	egg yolks, beaten	2
1/2 cup	Olympic Natural Yogurt	125 mL
	salt	
	pepper	
	flour	
	olive oil	

Cut bread, green pepper and cheese into 1" squares and skewer alternately with tomatoes. Blend egg yolks with yogurt, salt and pepper. Dip each kebab into mixture, sprinkle with flour and fry in hot olive oil until golden brown. Drain well before serving. Serves 4.

Fluffy Stuffy Potatoes

Nothing stuffy about these!

3	baking potatoes	3
1/2 cup	Olympic Natural Yogurt	125 mL
3	green onions, chopped	3
	salt	
	pepper	
2 tbsp.	parmesan cheese, grated	30 mL

Bake potatoes at 350° F. (180°C) for one hour, or until done. Cut a thick lengthwise slice from the top of each potato and scoop hot potato pulp into mixing bowl. Add yogurt, green onions, salt and pepper and mix well. Spoon mixture into shells rounding tops. Sprinkle with parmesan cheese. Place in shallow baking pan and bake at 425° F. (220°C) for fifteen minutes or until hot and lightly browned. Serves 3.

Note: These can be made up to two days in advance. To cook straight from the refrigerator, bake for 20 to 25 minutes.

Variations:
1. Add 1/2 cup (125 mL) fresh or frozen broccoli to the yogurt mixture.
2. Mix 3/4 cup (175 mL) chicken stock, 1/2 cup (125 mL) finely chopped onion and 3 cloves minced garlic in a saucepan and bring to a boil over medium heat. Simmer uncovered ten minutes. Add the pulp from the potatoes along with 1-1/2 tsp. (7 mL) paprika and 1/8 tsp. (.5 mL) cayenne pepper along with 1 cup (250 mL) yogurt and mix well. Stuff the potato mixture back into the shells, sprinkle with parmesan cheese and place back in the oven for 10 minutes.

Deluxe Baked Mushrooms

A pleasant change!

24	whole mushrooms	24
4	green onions, chopped	4
1/2 cup	olive oil	125 mL
2 tbsp.	lemon juice	25 mL
1/4 cup	parsley	60 mL
1 tsp.	paprika	5 mL
2 tbsp.	flour	25 mL
1 cup	chicken broth	250 mL
1/2 cup	Olympic Natural Yogurt	125 mL
1 tbsp.	cornstarch	15 mL
	salt	
	pepper	
1/4 cup	cracker crumbs	50 mL

Saute mushrooms and green onions lightly in 1/4 cup (50 mL) olive oil. Sprinkle with lemon juice, parsley and paprika. Pour into casserole. Add 1/4 cup (50 mL) olive oil to the pan and blend in the flour to make a paste on medium heat. Add chicken broth slowly while stirring to make a sauce. Add cornstarch, salt and pepper to yogurt and mix well. Gradually add the hot mixture to the yogurt, a spoonful at a time, mixing well until about 1/2 cup (125 mL) has been added. Slowly add the yogurt mixture back into the hot mixture blending well. Pour over the mushrooms and sprinkle with cracker crumbs. Cover and refrigerate overnight. The next day bake at 325° F. (160°C) for 45 minutes. Serves 5.

Top a baked potato with Olympic Natural Yogurt and chives instead of sour cream!

Cheesy Onions

Another favorite!

4 cups	sliced onions	1 L
2 tbsp.	olive oil	30 mL
2 tbsp.	flour	30 mL
	salt and pepper	
3/4 cup	onion liquid	175 mL
3/4 cup	grated Cheddar cheese	175 mL
1 cup	Olympic Natural Yogurt	250 mL
1 tsp.	cornstarch	5 mL
1/2 cup	bread crumbs	125 mL

Cook the sliced onions in salted boiling water for ten minutes. Drain, retaining 3/4 cup (175 mL) of the liquid. Put the onions in a buttered baking dish. In the original pot, add the oil and flour and stir to make a smooth paste. Remove from heat. Add salt, pepper, onion liquid and cheese. Stir until cheese is melted. Add cornstarch to yogurt, blending well. Gradually add some of the hot mixture to the yogurt then add all the yogurt mixture to the cheese mixture. Pour sauce over the onions and top with bread crumbs. Bake covered at 375° F. (190°C) for 30 minutes. Serves 6.

Winter Squash

Colorful and quick!

2 lbs.	Banana or Hubbard squash	1 kg
1/2 cup	Olympic Natural Yogurt	125 mL
1/2 tsp.	dill weed	2 mL
1	green onion, finely sliced	1
	black pepper	

Cut squash into 1-1/2" cubes. Pare off tough rind. Combine in saucepan with water and salt and cook until tender. Drain and toss gently with yogurt, dill weed and onions. Sprinkle with black pepper and serve at once. Serves 6.

Broccoli with Yogurt Sauce

Even those who don't like "trees" will love this!

3 cups	broccoli florets, steamed	750 mL
2 cups	Olympic Natural Yogurt	500 mL
2 tsp.	flour	10 mL
1/2 tsp.	pepper	2 mL
2	cloves garlic, minced	2
1/2 tsp.	Worcestershire Sauce	2 mL
1 tbsp.	lemon juice	15 mL
1 cup	Cheddar cheese, grated	250 mL

Grease a casserole dish and add broccoli. Combine yogurt, flour, pepper, garlic, Worcestershire Sauce, lemon juice and Cheddar in a separate bowl. Pour over the broccoli. Bake at 350° F. (180°C) for approximately 20 to 25 minutes or until heated through. Serves 4.

Potato Cakes

These originated in Finland!

1	onion	1
4 cups	potatoes, peeled and grated	1 L
2	eggs, lightly beaten	2
3 tbsp.	flour	45 mL
	salt	
1/3 cup	Olympic Natural Yogurt	75 mL
1/4 cup	olive oil	60 mL
	Mozzarella cheese	
	parsley, chopped	

Mix onion and potatoes in mixing bowl. Add eggs, flour, salt and yogurt. Beat until well blended. Heat 2 tbsp. olive oil in large skillet until very hot. Drop large spoonfuls of mixture into skillet and cook over moderately high heat until browned on bottom. Add more olive oil if needed. Turn and sprinkle liberally with parsley and Mozzarella cheese and brown the other side. Serve immediately. Serves 4.

Saucy Green Beans

Substitute any kind of beans from your garden!

1 lb.	fresh green beans	500 g
2 tbsp.	chopped onion	30 mL
2 tbsp.	butter	30 mL
1/4 cup	Olympic Natural Yogurt	60 mL
2 tsp.	cornstarch	10 mL
1/4 cup	mayonnaise	60 mL
1 tbsp.	Dijon mustard	15 mL
1/4 tsp.	salt	1 mL

Cook beans in salted water until tender. Cook onion in butter until soft. Add beans. Combine yogurt, cornstarch, mayonnaise, Dijon and salt. Add to beans and heat just until hot. Do not boil. Serves 4.

Tasty Beets

Um, um good!

5	medium fresh beets	5
2 tbsp.	butter	30 mL
1 tbsp.	flour	15 mL
2 tbsp.	vinegar	30 mL
1 tbsp.	sugar	15 mL
1/4 tsp.	salt	1 mL
1 tbsp.	dill weed	15 mL
1/8 tsp.	pepper	.5 mL
1 tbsp.	cornstarch	15 mL
1/2 cup	Olympic Natural Yogurt	125 mL

Cook beets and cut into shoestring pieces. Melt butter and blend in flour. Cook over low hat until mixture is smooth and bubbly. Remove from heat. Add vinegar, sugar, salt, dill weed and pepper. Heat to boiling stirring constantly. Boil for 1 minute. Stir in beets and heat through. Add cornstarch to yogurt and mix thoroughly. Heat through over low heat and pour over hot beets. Serves 4.

Zucchini Supreme

Once you try this you will be planting extra zucchini!

3	medium zucchini, sliced	3
1/3 cup	Olympic Natural Yogurt	75 mL
2 tbsp.	butter	30 mL
1 tbsp.	Parmesan cheese, grated	15 mL
1/2 tsp.	salt	2 mL
1/8 tsp.	paprika	.5 mL
1/2 tsp.	oregano	2 mL
1	egg yolk	1
1 tbsp.	chives, chopped	15 mL
	bread crumbs	

Simmer zucchini in a small amount of water for 6 to 8 minutes. Drain and set aside. In a saucepan combine yogurt, butter, grated Parmesan, salt, paprika and oregano. Stir over low heat until hot. Remove from heat and stir in egg yolk and chives. Add zucchini. Put in baking dish, sprinkle with bread crumbs, dot with butter and sprinkle with more cheese. Brown under broiler. Serves 4.

Asparagus Spears with Horseradish Sauce

May be served hot, warm or cold!

1/2 cup	Olympic Natural Yogurt	125 mL
1 tbsp.	prepared horseradish	15 mL
	salt and pepper	
1/4 cup	Cheddar cheese, grated	60 mL
1/2 tsp.	hot mustard powder	2 mL
1/4 cup	white wine	60 mL
1 lb.	fresh asparagus	500 g
3	eggs, boiled 8 minutes, chopped	3
	parsley, chopped	

Whisk together yogurt, horseradish, salt, pepper, cheddar, mustard and white wine. Set aside. Snap bottoms off asparagus and steam until just tender. Arrange on serving plate, top with chopped eggs and spoon sauce over the top. Garnish with chopped parsley. Serves 4.

Saffron Asparagus

Saffron, the Queen of Spices!

1 cup	Olympic Natural Yogurt cheese	250 mL
1 tsp.	Dijon mustard	5 mL
1 tsp.	liquid honey	5 mL
1/8 tsp.	saffron	.5 mL
1/2 tsp.	cumin	1 mL
1 lb.	fresh asparagus, cooked	500 g

To make yogurt cheese, let yogurt sit in a sieve for half an hour or so until liquid has drained out. Combine yogurt cheese with mustard, honey, saffron and cumin. Mix well and refrigerate until needed. Serve over asparagus. Serves 4.

Savory Spinach

I ate twice as much as I intended to!

1 lb.	fresh spinach	500 g
1	onion, finely chopped	1
1/4 cup	butter	60 mL
1 cup	Olympic Natural Yogurt	250 mL
	salt and pepper	

Cook spinach until wilted using only the water that clings to the leaves. Saute onion in butter until tender. Drain spinach and add to onion. Saute for 5 minutes and remove from heat. Add salt and pepper to yogurt and pour over spinach. Serves 4.

Use Olympic Natural Yogurt as a mouth wash!

Brussels Sprouts Casserole

Dazzle your family at Thanksgiving dinner!

1-1/2 lb.	brussels sprouts, steamed	750 g
1 cup	tomatoes, stewed	250 mL
1/2 cup	Cheddar cheese, grated	125 mL
1 cup	Olympic Natural Yogurt	250 mL
2 tbsp.	flour	30 mL
1/4 cup	almonds, chopped and browned	60 mL

Arrange brussels sprouts in oiled casserole and cover with tomatoes. Mix grated cheese, yogurt and flour together and spoon over sprouts. Cover and bake at 350° F. (180°C) for 15 minutes. Garnish with chopped almonds. Serves 4 to 6.

Raita

This is an East Indian dish usually served with curries. As well as adding color to the meal it complements and provides cooling relief from the hotter, more dominant dishes!

1	medium cucumber	1
2	medium tomatoes	2
1 tbsp.	onion, finely chopped	15 mL
1 cup	Olympic Natural Yogurt	250 mL
1/4 cup	parsley, freshly chopped	60 mL
1 tsp.	fresh cilantro, chopped	5 mL
1 tsp.	cumin	5 mL
1/4 tsp.	fennel seeds	1 mL

Peel cucumber and remove seeds. Cut into thin slices. Core tomatoes, and cut into 1/2" (1 cm) cubes. Toss with cucumbers, and onion. Drain off any liquid. Add yogurt, parsley, cilantro, cumin and fennel. Refrigerate until ready to serve. Serves 4.

Baked Aubergine (Eggplant)

This is one of the easiest and tastiest ways to prepare eggplant!

3 tbsp.	olive oil	45 mL
1	onion, chopped	1
1 lb.	eggplant, unpeeled	500 g
1 cup	Olympic Natural Yogurt	250 mL
3 tbsp.	fresh mint, chopped	45 mL
2 cloves	garlic, minced	2
1/4 tsp.	salt	1 mL
	freshly ground pepper	
	paprika	

Cook onion in oil until softened. Remove onion and set aside. Cut eggplant into 1/4" (5 mm) slices. Brush remaining oil on eggplant slices and arrange in single layer on baking sheet. Bake at 400°F. (200°C) until tender and soft, about 15 minutes. In ungreased casserole dish, alternate layers of eggplant and onions. Combine yogurt, mint, garlic salt and pepper and drizzle over eggplant slices. Sprinkle with paprika. Bake at 350° F. (180°C) until hot and bubbly, about 15 minutes. Serves 6.

Artichokes with Yogurt Hollandaise

A fun way to start a meal!

4	artichokes	4
1 tbsp.	olive oil	15 mL
3	lemon slices	3
1	bay leaf	1
1 clove	garlic, minced	1 clove
1 tsp.	salt	5 mL
6	peppercorns	6
	Yogurt Hollandaise (see Appetizers, Dips & Sauces)	

Wash artichokes and cut off stem at base. Remove small bottom leaves and using a scissors, trim tips from leaves. Cut a 1" slice across top. In a deep casserole dish, stand artichokes upright. Add boiling water to measure 3" and add olive oil, lemon slices, bay leaf, garlic, salt and peppercorns. Cook in microwave for 15 minutes or until base is pierced easily. Drain upside down. Serve with Hollandaise Sauce for dipping.

To eat, pull outside leaves off, one by one, dip in sauce and slide the fleshy part between the teeth. Discard leaf and go on to the next. It is quite an experience the first time you eat an artichoke. When you reach the heart, discard the middle thistle part and savor the heart using the rest of the Hollandaise Sauce. Serves 4.

Stuffed Courgettes (Zucchini)

Use zucchinis about 5" (13 cm) long and 1-1/2" (4 cm) thick!

12	zucchini	12
1/2 lb.	lean ground beef	250 g
1 cup	rice, cooked	250 mL
1/2 cup	Olympic Natural Yogurt	125 mL
2 tbsp.	parsley, chopped	30 mL
2 tbsp.	pine nuts	30 mL
1/2 tsp.	cinnamon	2 mL
	black pepper	
1-1/2 cups	chicken stock	375 mL
2 cups	Olympic Natural Yogurt	500 mL
2 tbsp.	cornstarch	30 mL
2 cloves	garlic, minced	2 cloves
1 tbsp.	fresh mint, chopped	15 mL

Trim the stems from the zucchini and cut a lengthwise piece off each for the "lid" about 1/2" thick. Scoop out the flesh from the middle. Combine the meat, rice, yogurt, parsley, pine nuts, cinnamon and pepper and mix well. Stuff the hollowed out courgettes with this mixture and place in a casserole dish. Bring the stock to a boil and pour over the zucchini. Cover and bake at 350° F. (180°C) for 1 hour. Mix the cornstarch with the yogurt and pour over the zucchini. Cook, uncovered for another 20 minutes. Just before serving, melt the butter and add the garlic and mint and cook for about 1 - 2 minutes. Pour over the zucchini and serve immediately. Serves 6.

Mushroom Strudel

A very filling vegetarian dish! Try substituting fennel seeds for poppy seeds!

Filling		
1 lb.	mushrooms, sliced	500 g
1 cup	cream cheese	250 mL
1 tsp.	salt	5 mL
	pepper, freshly grated	
1/2 tsp.	dill	2 mL
	ground caraway	
1/2 cup	sour cream	125 mL
1/2 cup	Olympic Natural Yogurt	125 mL
1 cup	fine bread crumbs	250 mL
1/4 cup	parsley, chopped	60 mL
1	scallions, minced	2
	juice from 1 lemon	
10	filo pastry leaves	10
1 cup	butter, melted	250 mL
2 tbsp.	poppy seeds	30 mL

Steam the mushrooms and drain. Cut the cream cheese into the hot mushrooms, tossing until the cheese melts. Add remaining filling ingredients and mix well.

To assemble, lay a leaf of filo pastry flat and brush with butter. Add another leaf on top and brush with more butter. Continue to stack the leaves until you have a pile of 5. Spread half the filling across the width of the leaves over a 3 - 4" space and roll up tightly. Brush the top with butter and sprinkle 1 tbsp. (15 mL) of poppy seeds. Transfer to a buttered tray. Repeat this ritual to make the second roll. Slash each roll into thirds on the diagonal. Bake at 375° F. (190°C) for 25 minutes. Serve hot. Serves 6.

METRIC CONVERSIONS

Volume

Measure	Approximate Replacement
1/8 tsp.	.5 mL
1/4 tsp.	1 mL
1/2 tsp.	2 mL
1 tsp.	5 mL
1 tbsp.	15 mL
1/4 cup	60 mL
1/3 cup	75 mL
1/2 cup	125 mL
2/3 cup	150 mL
3/4 cup	185 mL
1 cup	250 mL
1-3/4 cups	425 mL
2 cups	500 mL
2-1/2 cups	625 mL
3 cups	750 mL
4 cups	1 L
5 cups	1.2 L
6 cups	1.5 L
8 cups	2 L
12 cups	3 L

Mass

1/2 lb.	250 g
1 lb.	500 g
2 lb.	1000 g
2 lb.	1 Kg

Oven Temperature

300° F.	150°C
325° F.	160°C
350° F.	180°C
375° F.	190°C
400° F.	200°C
425° F.	220°C
450° F.	230°C

INDEX

Bread, Biscuits & Muffins contd.

Breakfasts and Brunches

Cakes

Cookies

Desserts

Dips

Dressings

Fish & Seafood

Meat Dishes

Pasta

Poultry

Rice

Salad

Salad, contd.

Sauces

Soup

Soup. contd.

Vegetables